The Perfect Time to Garden …

Is Not necessarily right now

Kevin K. Napora

The Perfect time to Garden… is Not necessarily right now.
ISBN-13: 978-1493791125
ISBN-10: 1493791125

Edited by Justine Jenkins-Crumb, Coordinator of the Master Gardener programme at the University of Alberta, Devonian Botanic Garden.

Second Editing by Lesley Bowness and Heidi Lacey.

Design editing by Cara Bedford, Marketing Director for Salisbury Landscaping

Printed by Priority Printing Ltd.

Includes bibliographical references.

Cover Design by Karley Cunningham

Back Cover and Author's Picture by Ryan Hidson

All book Photography by

Kevin K. Napora, B.Sc. Agric., Master Gardener

To Rob, this book would never have been attempted without your support and encouragement

Forward

I met Kevin Napora on a particularly bright and sunny summer day several summers ago while traipsing through his yard, which was a part of the Edmonton Horticulture Society Garden Show. It was my first time attending this annual two-day event, which highlights a number of different styles of gardens in the Edmonton area. I liked Kevin's garden right away. I liked its informality, the variety of color and plant material, its unassuming flow. Of course, the most interesting feature in the garden that day was Kevin. Here was a man who clearly loved what he was doing, loved talking about it, and loved sharing information.

Then I realized his lush, vibrant yard was only three years old. Three years old? How was that possible? It had the look of a garden years in the making. How had he done it? I couldn't even form the questions. I walked away impressed but baffled.

A few months later, my partner and I hired Kevin to landscape our small backyard. That's when I really got to know him. His good humor, professionalism, and passion for growing things was evident at every step. We were clear what we didn't want: no deck, no grass. We wanted trees, roses, and a hint of whimsy. He delivered on every account, along with a list of instructions on how to maintain and grow our yard. That's when I panicked. *When* do I fertilize? *When* do I prune? *When* do I add compost?

So when Kevin announced he was writing this book, I was very happy. Finally, a book that takes into account our northern climate and short growing season, that tells us what we need to do in the garden throughout the year, step by step, clearly and simply. And he didn't leave out the whimsy.   Heidi Lacey (Dear friend)

CONTENTS

Introduction

Tall, lanky, yet exuberant and still in university, I finally landed my first job in my career as a gardener on the zone 3 prairies. I was fortunate enough to have been paired with an experienced hand. Filled with energy and excitement for the job, I couldn't wait to get started and get things done. But over the course of that summer, I learned two main things: one, gardening is hard work and two, everything is about timing. Every time I wanted to do something, or made a suggestion, the answer was either it was too late or too early. Inevitably, whatever needed to be tackled should have been done in the spring. Moving down the task list, the next priority would have to wait for the coming month, and so on. Now that I am in my forties my answers are often the same to similar questions. Gardening is still a lot of work but by doing the right job at the right time you can turn constant defeat into a rewarding experience and a beautiful garden.

Now, I know that I have just made a huge gaff in saying that gardening is work. I am supposed to tell you that it is fun, easy, fast, and guaranteed. Perhaps, I should even tell you it can be done for free, ideally, but in reality you have to actively go outside and do something. Therein lies the problem: what, and when? My partner and I have quite a large garden that has been in quite a few garden tours and magazines. Through every tour I can't tell you how many people have asked me the same question, "How many hours do you spend in the yard every week?" The truth is maybe 2-3 hours; however, a good portion of that is enjoying a glass of wine while strolling through the garden. A garden really shouldn't take more than 1-2 hours per week to maintain.

My own garden, even though overrun with colour, is easy to maintain

What I find to be the largest problem with a good portion of gardeners is that they let a small problem explode into a monumental crisis. A little quack grass turns into a lawn inside the daylilies, or the irises become over run with dandelions. Later as the summer progresses, there you

sit for hours attempting to pull these weeds out only to sadly break the roots. Once the roots are broken, these end up only coming back week after week. People then don't see results, become defeated, and then eventually convert the garden into a gravel bed.

The goal of this book is to direct you to do the right job, at the correct time of the year to avoid wasted effort, time and sweat. The book is arranged chronologically from spring through fall. Details are provided so that you are informed of what to do week by week. Each month has an over-all aspiration and then each month is divided into 4 weeks. Week one is day 1-7, Week two is 8-14, Week three is 15-22, and week four is 23-30.

As it should be, the spring and fall demand the most effort yet this will result in a summer of fun: full of free evenings to enjoy easy weekends with family and friends. (There - that should make my publicist happy.)

Background

I was very fortunate to have entered into the gardening world when I did as I was right in the middle of the transition period from the European trained gardeners to the new scientific way of looking at the world. I basically had negligible exposure as a kid growing up to the whole world of plants. In grade 12 I had to pick a career. Once a week, my mom made me go out and weed our little condo garden and while I was sitting in the dirt I realized that I truly enjoyed this chore. The next day I went to my guidance counsellor and said I want to be a gardener (much to my mom's horror as she wanted me to engineer bridges). My counsellor had no idea how to find gardening in the university catalogue; as a result, I ended up in the Department of Agriculture studying plant science, quite by accident. I could just have easily ended up in Botany, had my counsellor thought of the word. To my benefit, just as I was entering University, the last of the hippies were leaving. I learned all about planting by the moon phases, listening to the whispers of the plants and being concerned for their feelings. I was even lucky enough to be able to sit in a seminar about cosmically infused soils. During the summer, I worked under all sorts of people who taught me the old sayings about what the wind directions were to have meant; three fogs in January bringing wet weather in summer, or roses not liking to be touched by metal, etc. But most importantly I was taught that the bulk of gardening knowledge is passed down and experienced.

My most favourite job was working as a herb gardener at the Devonian Botanic Garden near Edmonton, Alberta. For two hours every Monday morning, my boss would walk me through the garden and he would easily talk about 50 plants in Latin. "Kill this one, not that one", "Don't touch that one or you will kill us all". Stuff like that. For the rest of the week I continued working and finishing everything using my trusty fork, hoe and dandelion digger. To this day I can still rattle off many of the names. I loved that job, except when a cow bird kept trying to land on me.

By the time I finished university much of the landscape had changed. Horticulture became a science. Students focused on the biochemistry, molecular structures and active ingredients. By then as well, most of the district horticulturalists had been eliminated and the greenhouses for the university, city and province were closing. Within two more years, the massive

annual planting beds around the University were not only gone but were grassed over. Subsequently, since there weren't any jobs available I needed to start my own business.

Gardening changed massively. New tools had come and gone, pesticides and herbicides went from darlings to devils, and gardens went from food, to flowers, then shrubs, and now to food again. Yet really, these changes were minor. The biggest change I noticed was people discovering or re-discovering that gardening encompassed a philosophy. Unfortunately, this philosophy that in the past was deeply woven into every gardening task seems now to be missing. That passed down experience has been forgotten.

I am going to step back just for a second to talk about my philosophy about gardening and its importance. I have taught many courses over the years and I am often seriously criticized about my teaching the topic of integrated pest management. This method uses all techniques of good husbandry, cultural control, but also incorporates the responsible use of chemical control. Proper timely application of herbicides saves an exceptional amount of time and headaches. Over the last couple of decades, people are people, and if 50ml is good then a litre is better. To be fair to the organic gardeners' movement, there has been way too much use and wastage of chemical; however, it is very easy to get caught up in the world of black and white and not appreciate the benefit of all the greys. Thoughtful, careful use of pesticides and herbicides can alleviate so many problems while gardening. What I find the most alarming, though, is that new gardeners are often scared off because, instead of being encouraged, they are filled with fears. This book will deal primarily with cultural practices, when and to some extent how, but also effective and timely use of other control methods.

Through human history, we have been surrounded by nature. We had to listen and watch at all times to every sign as our very survival depended on what we learned. We were completely integrated into a living, changing environment and to this day the outside world can penetrate deep into what makes us human. People have become completely disassociated from nature. A good example just last week I saw a teenage girl in a plant store who saw a gnat (.5mm) crawling on a table. She freaked out, insisting that her sister had to run from the other side of the store to squish it.

When I meet someone who is interested in gardening I get completely ebullient because that person is going to be outside. She is going to hear the poplar leaves rustle in the breeze, see a circle of birds have a giant squabble, and smell rich soil that

makes your mouth water. The most important thing is that she will be outside and will experience nature. So the most important thing to me is to make it as easy as possible to be outside. If you like fresh food – let's grow food; if you like bouquets – let's grow flowers. People are on a continuum of learning and a good gardener understands how the world grows and matures.

I have spent years training new gardeners not only techniques but the importance of noticing. In this book, let's walk through the garden at

the start of every week and let's talk about the different techniques needed and the times that they are to be applied.

We will find out the whys. Once you understand the why then you can choose your own path depending on what you want to achieve.

My goal is that at the end of the year you will have spent time outside, enjoyed the summer, and be baffled at how quickly the season has passed.

Additional Reading Material:

Evans, Clinton L. (2002). *The War on Weeds in the Prairie West. An Environmental History.* Calgary, Alberta, Canada: University of Calgary Press.

Louv, Richard (2005). *Last Child in the woods. Saving our children from Nature-deficit disorder.* Chapel Hill, North Carolina: Algonquin Books.

Martin, Carol (2000). *A History of Canadian Gardening.* Toronto, Ontario: McArthur and Company.

Tomkins, Peter, & Christopher Bird (1973). *The Secret Life of Plants.* New York, NY: Avon Books.

Steiner, Rudolf (1993). *Spiritual Foundations for the Renewal of Agriculture.* Kimberton Pennsylvania: Bio Dynamic Farming and Gardening Association, Inc.

MARCH

Some years it takes winter a little longer to move along than others

Week 1 in March – Pruning of larger branches (>2 inches)

The end of winter is marked with the swelling of the poplar buds. This is usually around the first week of March and begins your exciting adventure into the gardening world.

The Perfect Time to Garden is...

Pruning of larger tree branches or removal of large stems of shrubs usually begins now. You can do this type of pruning throughout the winter, and large pruning companies do. But for a homeowner, why prune in the middle of winter when it is minus thirty? It is far better to prune in early spring when it is warmer and sunnier.

There are many reasons to prune but the primary reasons are the 3Ds: Dead, Damaged, and Diseased. To this I add one more D, Dangerous.

It is often difficult to see dead branches so usually we prune these ones out in the first week in June. But it is easy to see broken or cracked branches or Shubert Chokecherries covered in thick black knots. I have, for a some time now, added dangerous branches: branches that rub against the house, or drupe down to potentially poke out eyes or rip clothing. These have to be removed as well.

There are a myriad number of pruning tools but your primary tool for large branches is a long pruning saw and a folding pruning saw. Do not use a saw that cuts dimensional wood. The teeth are far too fine for a tree cut. If you happen to have

a reciprocating saw you can buy blades meant for tree pruning. You will need a ladder; the best being a 3 legged pruning ladder (also called an orchard ladder).

Pruners, Loppers, Pruning Saw, Folding Saw

Additional tools are a pole pruner and extending pruner

Now that we have the tools we need to know the rules:

This rule is absolute: Never cut more than a third of the tree or shrub. This, however, only applies to living wood. If half of your tree is dead then you can remove all of it plus the one third of the live growth. You won't have much of a tree left but it is feasible. The tree has evolved to withstand and react to both minor and major injuries. A bear rubbing against the bark, or a moose knocking off one of its branches, is a minor part of being in the forest with animals. But if more than that happens, then the tree or shrub has to react as if it is being under attack from disease, pests, or worse, humans. And the tree goes into survival mode and produces hundreds of little branches to create a witch's broom affect or hundreds of suckers, produced at ground level near the base of the tree. The result is a horrible looking tree or shrub that will be susceptible to diseases or winter injuries.

Don't prune Maples or Birch before June and it is illegal to cut Elm trees from April 1 to October 31. Maples and Birch bleed all over the places and then the sap attracts ants and aphids. Elm trees are susceptible to Dutch Elm Disease which has wiped out elm trees across North America. The exception to this devastation is Edmonton, Alberta which has the largest stand of adult elm trees in North America. The inner city still has streets lined as if they were cathedrals. This sight is absolutely breathtaking in fall.

Another rule is that trees or shrubs grow either up or out. (This leads to a different rule of landscape design: plant the correct plant with the mature height and spread that you want.) People often don't believe this but plants have a pre-set height and spread, and plants want to reach those growth parameters. So if the plant is growing too tall and you cut off the top then it will grow quite fat. And same, if the plant is getting too wide for its space and you start trimming it, then it will start to get tall.

The next rule has to do with growth rates. Pruning in the spring (March) invigorates a tree and pruning in the summer (July) slows down a tree. So if you want to make your tree grow taller and wider then you prune in the winter and early spring. But if your tree has reached the size that you want it to be and you need to slow it down, then you will prune in the summer. This has to do with food storage. In the fall the tree, like a squirrel, has been storing food preparing for winter and getting ready to grow in the spring. So when you prune in spring the once dormant buds are activated and the tree grows more branches. But during the summer all of the food that was in the roots is now gone and the tree is relying on the leaves in the upper canopy to create food for the winter. If you remove branches, consequently leaves, in the summer there is less food returning to the roots in the winter. Hence slower growth the following year.

The penultimate rule is that you never cut the top of an evergreen e.g. a spruce (unless it has one of the D's) otherwise you will have to prune it every year thereafter. In fact most arborists will never cut the top of any tree. This is called topping. It causes tremendous hardship to a tree and results in all kinds of future problems.

And finally the last rule is never cut into the cambium. The cambium is basically a thin layer of skin underneath the bark that seals a cut. The cambium will create a protective layer over a wound to keep diseases from getting into the body of the tree and then slowly begins the process of covering the cut with new bark over the next few years.

It takes many years to seal over a bad cut

The great thing is that trees especially, and most large shrubs draw a perfect line to tell you where the cambium is. In general it is a few millimetres away from the trunk of the tree. To prune cut just a half centimetre away from it. Not further nor closer. If you cut too close then you may nick the cambium. If you cut too far then the plant will have to spend years trying to grow bark around the stub.

Another important technique is to make many cuts rather than one big giant cut. For example, if you have a fairly long branch that is sticking out and scratching the house then you start by sawing a line under the branch near the trunk make a one inch cut upwards at the bottom of the branch that you are cutting, about a centimetre from the bottom up. Then start by removing the part nearest to the house. Cut off a six foot section and then another until you are about four feet or so away from the trunk of the tree. Before you make that final cut though near the trunk just make sure that you have made that one inch cut underneath the branch that you are cutting. Then saw from the top of the branch down just outside of the cambium towards where you had created the small notch. The reason for this method is that sometimes if you just start cutting the top of the branch closest to the trunk the weight of the branch can be so heavy that it will then rip the bark all the way down the side of the trunk of the tree and create a massive wound. At this point there is nothing that can be done, except clean up the wound and maybe consider giving away your pruning tools

Evergreen Desiccation

Covering of Zone 4 evergreen material is critical at this time of the year. The snow is slowly melting and often crystallizes on the surface. Once the sun comes out it can be quite blinding for us, but for plants it can be deadly. Plants like Alberta spruce, Norway pines, cedars, or boxwood are not designed to be on the prairies and as soon as March comes the leaves become active. The problem though is the roots are still frozen. So as the sun comes out the leaves release the little bit of water that they still have but the roots cannot pump water back into them. The leaves then become sunburnt and turn brown. To prevent this sun damage cover the plants with a sun shade. In the fall all of the stores and greenhouses sell perennial blankets, or green shade pop up tents, or burlap fabric. All are great to cover the plants for the month until the snow is gone. Just a note, it is quite common for people to cover up their evergreens in November. Absolutely you can do this, it is much nicer to work in the warmth of November. But, if you were busy or on vacation you positively must cover them in the early spring to prevent sunburn.

Additional Reading Material:

Capon, Brian (2010). Botany for Gardeners (3rd Edition). Portland, Oregon: Timber Press.

Coombs, Duncan, Peter Blackburne-Maze, Martyn Cracknell, & Roger Bentley (1992). *The Complete Book of Pruning*. London, England: Ward Lock.

Week 2 in March - Snow removal along the front street

As the city blades the streets during the winter, snow is piled quite high, called windrows, along the boulevards. These wind rows are filled with salts, gravel bits, and garbage. As the snow melts it is important to shovel or sweep this debris into the street while the lawn is still frozen. Once the lawn starts to melt, the salts will get into the soil and destroy its growing potential. As well, the gravel bits will affect your mower, especially if you are using a reel (cylinder) mower.

On a small note, the soil is usually frozen completely during the morning. So this is also quite a good time to fix things in the yard. Once the sun comes out during the afternoon the ground can get too wet or squishy.

Seeding

This is generally the beginning of indoor seeding time. Some  seeds needed to have been started earlier but for the most part it begins with the seeding of tomatoes which begins this week around March 15. There are classes in all of the bigger greenhouses at this time, as well, books about seeding and different techniques are also available.

I don't plant in the thousands. I need a few of this and that. So my favourite method is to buy the little peat plugs. You soak them and in 30 seconds they puff up. You put your seed inside and in about a week they start to sprout. The greenhouses sell little troughs that sit on the window sill with a dome to keep the humidity up. Be mindful that you leave a space for heat to escape during the day.

If you have a little money, you can buy a florescent light designed to prevent your new babies from extending and stretching for light. This will cause them to be weak and often to fall over. The more light that you can give the seedlings in the initial stages will help them to create strong stems later on.

Over the next few weeks, you will repeatedly transplant them into slightly larger pots. The plants cannot go directly from a peat plug into a large pot. The soil often becomes water logged resulting in root rot. In mid-May, you will have to start moving your transplants outside during the day and inside at night to toughen them up and prepare them for life outside.

Week 3 in March – Peat moss to melt the snow

This is one of my favourite times in the spring. The snow is melting and generally it is starting to noticeably warm up. The migratory birds are just beginning to return from their winter holidays and there is a little bit of frolicking starting to happen amongst the branches. The problem is the frustration that you can't make things happen faster. But you can!

For your own personal sanity, snow at this time needs to disappear and the fastest way to do that is to spread peat moss on the snow. This can only be done on gardens that do not have a mulch, like bark or gravel. The peat moss absorbs heat on sunny days and increases the rate of melt. This accomplishes a couple of things. First, in May we spread and mix in peat moss to increase the organic content of the soil and help with aeration. By doing it now we can walk on the snow, thus not compacting wet soil later in spring. As well, we shift some of the work load forward. And second, young trees are very susceptible to sunscald. Their bark is very tender and the sun light bouncing off the snow can cause fairly severe sunburns (called sunscald) on their trunks. By spreading the peat moss on the snow you reduce the glare substantially.

A large garden would only need two 4 cubic foot bags of peat moss as you spread it quite thinly and evenly over the snow. You could substitute compost as well or lawn clippings provided that it is fine enough. The point of the peat moss is not to function as a nutrient source for the plant material; however, it will improve texture and water holding capacity. If you were to use compost, it would also provide some nutrient improvement. Peat moss is for opening up the soil, and increasing the organic matter. Peat moss has the added benefit of absorbing a vast amount of moisture to keep the soil more evenly moist. The big negative is when peat moss dries out. It becomes hydro-phobic. That is, it repels water and makes it more difficult to re-hydrate the soil during a dry spell in the middle of summer.

Snow Mould

Snow mould (*Typhula* spp.) is a fungus that thrives just as the snow is melting and spreads on the lawn. Most lawns are afflicted by the more common grey snow mould that is not overly

A quick 10 second sweep solves mould issues

destructive. Snow mould is easily controlled by sweeping the mould with a corn broom. The point is to break up the mycelium (the white webbing) so that the fungus can't kill the grass. Fungus can be a problem on newly planted lawns that don't have a strong enough root system to recover from the damage caused by the mycelium.

Week 4 in March – Prepping your Tools

Spring is coming, but it's not here yet. I am sure it has already snowed again, and it is probably minus fifteen as you are reading this. But for sure spring is coming. So this week is time to prep some of your tools.

I have always highly recommended that everyone buy a

grinding wheel, or at a bare minimum you need a good sharpening stone. Spades, shovels, and pruning blades all need to be in tip top shape. When you are in a gardening mood there is nothing worse than struggling with a pair of pruners just to cut the head off of a dandelion. Bringing your mowers into the lawn mower hospital to have the oil changed, new filters installed, and blades sharpened will make your lawn ever so happy.

If you have a reel mower (or cylinder mower) this is great time to sit on the deck with a cup of hot cocoa and sharpen each of the blades and oil the wheels.

There is quite a bit of pruning to come next week so definitely spend some time sharpening your pruning equipment. Also this is a great time to wash windows, and pull out the deck furniture. Yes, I can see that it is still snowing but if everybody put out their deck furniture then it would confuse old man winter into thinking it was time to take a snooze for a few months.

APRIL

April is marked by the buds of apple trees turning a soft fuzzy grey. An old saying is that you can begin working in the garden one week after Easter, which for the most part is usually true, except if you live in the northern parts of the Prairie Provinces. April is a fantastic time for taking gardening courses, spring

cleaning both inside and outside, bird watching, and just

heralding the sun and warmth.

Our primary focus in April is to clean. Pruning out of diseased material, corrective pruning, training of shrubs, and removal of dead debris from last year, are all of the tasks done in April.

For people in new developing neighbourhoods, I like to recommend being a good neighbour for a couple of weeks. I usually walk my dog every day and for the next couple of weeks I take a big garbage bag with me and pick up garbage as

I go. On the whole, it makes me feel good that I am doing something for the community and on a selfish note I don't have to look at garbage. You just may notice that in time other people will be walking around with garbage bags too. It's a feel good for everyone.

Week 1 in April – Fruit tree and shrub pruning (<2")

Fruit trees and shrubs can easily be done earlier in March but one of the main reasons it is recommended to be done now is that the wounds left from your cuts can become susceptible to drying out.

If you haven't pruned your fruit trees in a few years then have them professionally done first. Once they are done, it is much easier for you to keep up on the maintenance. First you need tools. Usually by now all of the hardware stores and greenhouses are already stocked so you can pop in and pick up a lopper and, if you can find one, an extendable hand pruner or pole pruner.

As with all things, in regard to pruning, you can't have it all. So you can prune for flowers, you can prune for fruit, or you can prune for form. This applies to all types of pruning be it for shrubs or trees. If you prune for flowers then you want long thin branches resulting in flowers along the stems. If you prune for fruit then you want stronger branches and fewer of them so that the fruit has room to grow and branches strong enough to support the weight. Most people opt for the form. They want a nice looking tree that doesn't crowd out the neighbour or drop fruit all over the sidewalk or driveway.

If you are pruning for flowers then you will want to prune at the end of May, otherwise if you prune now, then you will be cutting off all of your flowers. If you are pruning for form,

then you are actually hedging your tree and this is done in July. Pruning for fruit is done now.

The primary goal is to have an open space in the middle so that the plants "can breathe" and also so that pests and fungus can't easily hop from one leaf to the next. As well, the branches need to come out perpendicular from the branch rather than in a tight "V". This is so that the stem will be more flexible and be able to bend from the weight of the coming fruit.

The "can breathe" is in quotes because any scientist will tell you that the plant breaths from under the leaf in stomata. These words paint an important picture of the overall look when you are under the tree looking up. The branches can't be so thick that you can't see the sky. There should be a light airiness, a feeling of freedom. Often with years of pruning for form, especially with shrubs, the inside is as impenetrably tangled as the forest that surrounded Sleeping Beauty. Many homeowners have freaked right out when they hire an arborist to fix their tree and come home to see that there is nothing left. (One, he should have warned you and also he probably did take a bit too much out. Never forget the rule: Never more than a third.)

The last bit of pruning that you need to do is to clip the ends (heading back or pinching). Usually you take off only the last inch to six inches (2.5cm – 15cm). This encourages more small branches on the end and gives a bit fuller look without losing flowering and fruiting.

There are many great courses out there and excellent books to read as it is important to not guess. Below I have some general rules to follow as fruit trees will fruit on different parts of the tree. So you can't treat a cherry tree the same as you would an apple tree.

Apples and Pears

Fruit is either borne on spurs (living for 8 to 10 years) that form on branches two years old or older, although some fruit is also borne on new one year old wood. The general preference

is to prune for spurs, which are small knobby looking sticks about 3 inches tall (7cm). Remove twiggy growth so that the spurs can breathe and in April either head back or pinch back the one-year-old growth. In older orchards, the terminal growth was allowed to grow, however, in a backyard it is preferred to keep the tree in check. (New apple orchards have a different system of growth that works better for mechanical harvest. The trees are planted quite close together and look like columns.)

Prune to thin out entire branches (thinning) once the tree begins to bear, rather than cutting back. Poor fruit develops on thin branches, so proper thinning prevents crowding and shading of the fruit. The tree should be kept well-balanced by occasionally heading back those that are growing too vigorously. Well coloured fruit will develop when the centre of the tree is kept open allowing sunlight to reach the fruit.

Prune pears the same as apples insuring you have five to seven main branches again with a modified leader system. The spurs are shorter lived at six to eight years.

I have found over the years that apples also have a tendency to become biennial producers. That is, they will produce heavily one-year and then sparsely the next. After flowering, rub out up to half of the fruit buds if you find that you are in this cycle.

All apples are grafted on to hardy rootstock. And you must have two different apples to pollinate. The trees can be within two city blocks. To produce pear fruit, pears will cross with apples provided they flower at the same time; otherwise, you need two pear varieties.

Plums

Plums tend to be messy looking trees. They need a strong frame to support the long branches. Remove any weak or downward growing branches. The fruit is borne on lateral spurs (living for 6-8 years) that tend to be quite long. Thinning is important to prevent cross branching. Prune so that there is almost 2 feet (60 cm) of new growth on young bearing trees and about 1 foot (30 cm) on older trees. Plums can often have irregular bloom times which makes it difficult to find a cross pollinator. Plums do better when they cross pollinate with each other but just as pears and apples can cross pollinate so can plums and apricots, Nanking cherry or sand cherry will also work for the later blooming plums. Pollination is done by insects, mostly bees; therefore, if it is a cool spring with low insect activity you may have to pollinate by hand. This is why most people that grow plums will tell you they only get a crop every five years or so.

Apricot

Fruit is born on one year old shoots and on short spurs which carry most of the crop. Because the Spurs are short-lived (two to three years) pruning is used to encourage new growth not support the old-growth as in plums or apples. Therefore, apricots need heavier pruning, generally yearly. Pruning should be hard at least every three years. Apricot flower buds are sensitive to low temperatures producing flowers and fruit only if the minimum winter temperatures are above -32°C. Therefore, many years may go by before you get an apricot. Apricots bloom very early in the spring and it may be necessary to mulch the roots in the fall in order to delay bud break in the spring. Apricots are typical Prunus (this the name of their Family and are grouped with other trees like Mayday, chokecherry, or Nanking cherry) that will not tolerate wet feet. It would be best to have two different apricots for pollination but it is possible to use a Nanking cherry or a plum.

Cherries

 Cherries need a protected winter site and they will not tolerate poorly drained soils or excessive watering. Don't plant cherries near a lawn that will be irrigated, as the roots will not dry out. Many of the cherry varieties are self-fruiting and don't need a pollinator. Evans and Meteor are the most popular

varieties. Our cherries on the prairies, Zone 3, are classified as sour cherries although they are sold as sweet cherries. Sweet cherries grow in British Columbia, the American Coast, and quite maddeningly in Alaska. Sour cherries bear fruit on spurs on one year old shoots produced in the previous year.

Therefore cherries are pruned somewhat like apricots in that you want to encourage new growth. If you want your cherry tree for production, it is best not to create a tree but rather create a large shrub. For most people, though, the fruit is great for occasional eating and making a pie or two. Mostly, people want to create a small tree in the backyard.

Grape Vines

Grapes require a sunny south exposure for the best results. If a south exposure is not available look for a spot that is a heat trap in the garden.

The vines require some form of support. In some areas outside of the city it may be necessary to lay the vines down and cover them for the winter. Grapes ripen late August through September and a light frost will sweeten the fruit. Fruit is born on one year-old stems. Grape vines, therefore, should be pruned hard each year to encourage the development of a young lateral shoots. You should have two for pollination. The standard variety for the prairies is Valiant.

Cutting Back Early Risers

Another task that needs to be done at this time is to deal with your perennials from last year. The first week in April is often when we cut back last year's dead growth amongst plants that start to grow early. In the
middle of April we will be doing a full cut back of all of the perennials, but usually grasses, delphiniums, and daylilies can start to grow quite early and it makes it much more difficult to cut them back later in the month if new growth has started to push through last year's dead growth. I highly recommend cutting back these three plants now. This is of course if you didn't do a cut back in mid-October.

Week 2 in April – Mouse Poo

Usually by the second week in April most of the snow will have melted. For homes that are near a large field or forest, or acreages, from time to time when the snow melts you will discover tufts of grass in little piles. Over the course of the winter, mice have been running along under the snow eating your grass. They create little trails where they have been eating.

Some years are worse than others but usually the worst occurs in years when winter is late and the soil is kept warm during the fall. When winter finally arrives and dumps a heavy load of snow, this snow insulates the warm soil and creates perfect breeding conditions for mice.

The best thing that can be done is to rake up the dead grass. I strongly advise wearing a facemask, as you don't want to breathe in mice droppings. Certain types of mice can be infected with a virus that once breathed in by humans can cause severe reactions.

The grass will grow back on its own. But in late April we will be cleaning the sod, adding grass seed, and fertilizing. That will repair any damage created by the mice

Another unfortunate reality is mouse, bunny, and deer damage on shrubs and trees. In the late fall, we will be talking about how to protect your plants from damage, but being that you only just bought the book, I am going to assume that you didn't protect your plants last season. Unlike grass, shrubs and  trees sometimes don't recover. If an animal has eaten the bark all the way around the tree stem ("girdling"), the tree will die if you do nothing. As long as you have one finger width of bark, 1 inch (2.5cm), that is intact and running straight from the bottom to the top I have seen many young trees survive. They are severely stunted for a few years but they continue. If the tree or shrub is completely girdled then the remedy is to cut off the top above the girdled area and hope that new branches will form underneath. The idea is to encourage only one to three new stems to regrow and become your future plant.

In order to understand a bit how trees store food for the winter and regrow in the spring, we will delve a little bit into botany and how a tree works.

During the summer, plants use their leaves to create food. The leaves draw the water from the roots through the centre of the stem, branch, or tree trunk. In the fall, all of that food needs to be stored for the winter in the roots underground. The food, aka sugars, is sent from the leaves and down the outside of the stems in an area just underneath the bark called the phloem. The food is stored in the roots for the winter. In the early spring, starting in April, the food is sent back up through the centre of the plant into the leaf buds, which then sprout out.

Here is the problem with girdling. When I have been called in to look at an issue and I proceed to tell the homeowner that he or she must address this with severe pruning, many of them don't. What happens is the roots send all of their reserves back up into the canopy and the plant flowers and leaves out. To which the homeowner then goes "Thank goodness I didn't listen to that guy he knew absolutely nothing!" But by late summer there is a problem. The roots have been sending all of the water and all of the stored sugars up into the leaves but nothing is coming back down via the phloem. So slowly the roots start dying off. For younger trees they will start to turn yellow in August and often be dead by September. For larger older trees they may take two years to die.

The remedy is to cut off the upper dead parts. In the spring, a vast amount of sugars will be forced to move from the roots up into the canopy but the plant will quickly discover that most of itself is missing. As a reaction all of the latent buds below the girdled area will be called into action and the plant will create new stems. If you trim them down into one or three stems then they will grow unbelievably quickly. If however the mice or rabbits girdled too low then there will be no hope for the new plant. This is also the same for shrubs. Unfortunately some shrubs will go into hyper growth and create literally hundreds of little stems called suckers. This can take a number of years before the plant calms down and realizes that it is not going to die. Some species like French Lilac or Schubert chokecherries will continue producing suckers for their entire lives.

There are some other remedies as well and can be found in any good books on tree pruning.

Week 3 in April – Cutting back perennials.

In the middle of April, the sun starts to shine and warm up the soil. And as a result, your little perennials will start to wake up and start to send out new shoots.

Just a quick jargon review. Shrubs and trees are plants that tend to have woody stems and the new growth usually comes from the ends of the branches. You will notice that trees don't have leaves that come from the ground but way up at the top of the tree. Perennials are different in that every year the new growth starts again from the ground. You will need to remove the old dead stems every year. Annuals, which we are not really going to talk about much in this book, are plants that die completely ever year. For annuals, e.g. petunias and marigolds, you will need to go to the store and buy them or reseed in spring.

There are literally thousands of perennials, and over the years I have learned that most people don't actually know the names of most of the plants that they own. They know them through stories. For example, a peony is described as the plant with the big pink flowers that fall down and attract ants. Delphiniums are said to be the tall blue flowers that break in the wind. Or my favourite story, goutweed is the green and white groundcover that their great aunt Selma gave them because they couldn't kill it. Here is the problem; how do you take care of something when you don't know what it is?

I have broken all perennials into three groups. Remember this is only for perennials. This does not include shrubs and trees.

Creeping Jenny - Groundcover

The first group is ground covers.

Ground covers are perennials that grow flat on the

ground.

They can be of all different heights. Some groundcovers like woolly thyme might be only a centimeter high while Bergenia might be 10" tall (25cm) or more.

Groundcovers are quite easy. You do nothing with them except to use a pair of hedge clippers to remove the dead flowers. I usually take the back end of a rake (turn the rake upside down) to brush out the dead leaves. There are a couple of exceptions. Goutweed (*Aegopodium podograria 'Variegatum'*) and Lily of the Valley (*Convallaria majalis*) should be cut to the ground.

Bergenia 'Eroica'

For homeowners new to gardening you will notice that out of nowhere I just started using Latin. In the gardening world, the use of scientific nomenclature is used commonly by gardeners as there often isn't an English word for many of the new introductions from around the world. As you get better and better in growing plants you will discover that many plants have quite a few English names, which will cause a fair bit of confusion. Old plant species brought over from England can often have five or more different names here in North America. So when you go into a greenhouse to purchase a plant, it is just easier and more accurate to purchase a plant using its Latin name, as there can only be one approved scientific name per plant.

If you are considering dabbling into herbalism and wanting to start creating healing teas etc. please learn your Latin and buy the correctly named plant. There are many examples of people in the hospital who bought the wrong plant and poisoned themselves.

The second group is mounding plants.

These are plants that grow into a mound shape. With these ones I recommend cutting back your plants to about 6" tall (15 cm) and shaping them into a ball shape. The reason for this is that the plants often have a thicker lower branch, or crown, and from this crown comes the new buds.

Euphorbia polychroma - Cushion Spurge

So if you were to cut the plant to the ground you would cut off the new buds. Good examples are the coral bells (*Heuchera*), cushion spurge (*Euphorbia*), and ornamental grass blue fescue (*Festuca glauca*). If you pull back

Festuca glauca - Blue Fescue

the basal leaves you will see the buds at the very base along the stems.

Here I would use my hand pruners, also called secateurs, to shape the plants.

The final group is the uprights.

Almost all of the other perennials fall into this group. You will find with this group that the perennials come straight out of the ground and grow straight up. This group includes the most common of perennials, example, peonies, delphiniums, lilies, tulips, or the tall upright grasses like Karl Forester grass, or ribbon grass. I recommend cutting these down to one or two inches (2.5cm to

5cm). For myself, I actually cut them right to the ground. There are a couple of exceptions. Irises have a thick root that runs along the surface of the soil. The dead leaves need to be cut down to about 2 inches (5cm) above the thick root. Daylilies, as well, have a little stub at soil

level that you shouldn't cut into. So for these I recommend 2 inches (5cm) above the soil.

Long ago when

I was a kid the recommended

Daylilies above and Irises below: cut at 2"

height to cut plants back to was six to eight inches (15cm to 20cm). I highly do not recommend this practice. If you were to go out in March and look at the perennials, you would see that the snow melts around the perennial and is exposing the core to the cold. If you had cut back your perennials to the ground then the snow would have continued to insulate and protect the crowns much later into the spring.

Cutting back perennials can be done with a knife or hand pruners (1" – 2")

Roses

A last small side note, for those of you who have roses, boxwoods, cedars or rhododendrons this is the time to pull off the rose caps and coverings. In the late fall of last year, the

tender zone fours and fives will have needed to have been covered and generally this is the time to take off these wraps. The idea with the wraps is not to have kept them warm but to protect the tender shrubs from drying out due to the wind or sunburn from the light reflecting off the snow (sunscald).

Additional Reading Material:

Williams, Sara (2013). *Creating the Prairie Xeriscape: Low Maintenance, water-efficient gardening.* Regina, Saskatchewan: Coteau Books.

Week 4 in April – Cleaning the Lawn of last year's dead grass

Aerating

I would imagine for the last couple of weeks now you have been bombarded with flyers from landscaping and gardening companies advertising about dethatching and aerating the lawn. Aerating is important for lawns but not necessary. Only lawns that see high traffic, example, if your yard is the yard that all of the neighbourhood kids play at on a daily basis, or you manage a soccer field, or build ice rinks, only then, do you need to aerate every year. Otherwise, you only need to aerate every three to five years. A proper aerating is when you pull out a core from the ground and leave an empty hole. Therefore, the spiked shoes that you wear around the yard to poke holes into the soil are not considered a good idea. What they do is in fact transfer the compaction deeper into the soil.

Most companies will core aerate and dethatch at the same time. My preference is to aerate the soil one week earlier and let the soil cores dry on top of the soil. Then the following week when you dethatch, the little "poops" disintegrate and enrich the soil. To get a good deep aeration, moisten the soil a couple days earlier so that the machine can sink into the grass and remove a deep plug. However, NEVER, aerate a wet soil. I will repeat this a few times through this book. If you put weight on to a wet soil you can destroy years of hard work by creating perfect compaction conditions. And it will take a surprisingly long time to repair the damage. To tell the difference between a wet soil and a moist one, you take a handful of soil and squeeze it. If water comes out then it is too wet. The best moisture level is when you squeeze the soil into a ball, open your hand, and then before your eyes the ball of soil crumbles. That would be the perfect time to begin aerating.

You can hire an expert or rent a machine and do it yourself. If you miss this time to aerate the lawn you can aerate again in October.

Dethatching

Unlike aerating, dethatching should be done every year once the thatch layer reaches a thickness of half an inch. Thatch is the build-up of decaying grass from past years. It is important to your sod because it insulates the roots from extreme heat and softens the impact from foot traffic. As the thatch breaks down it releases nutrients to the grass, basically acting as a slow release fertilizer. The problem though is that on the prairies it takes much longer than other places for the grass to disintegrate and return to the soil as nutrients. This is especially so if you fertilize the grass. What happens is the grass slowly starts to grow on top of the dead thatch. Over time the thatch layer and the lawn on top can grow so high that in one case I put my hand in between the grass layer and the soil layer and simply pushed through and separated the grass. The roots of the grass were no longer attached to the soil. As the thatch increases, it will take more and more water and fertilizer to keep the lawn looking good as well as potentially harbouring insect and disease problems. Water is also repelled as thatch can act the same as peat moss and become hydrophobic. When it dries it will slow the water from penetrating into the soil.

To check and see how much thatch you have, cut out a small square section of the lawn. Look at it, and if it is more than a half inch begin dethatching. Simply put the sod plug back in the lawn. The build-up of the thatch layer is encouraged by not picking up your lawn clippings or not cutting your grass frequently enough. Leaving long grass clippings on the lawn takes much longer to breakdown than regularly mowed smaller clippings. Over the last twenty years of mowing lawns, I have found that the best technique is to pick up lawn clippings until the second week in June. You can then stop, leave the clippings on the lawn for the summer (or compost them), and then start picking up again in September. I have found the clippings do not break down in time for winter.

The more you fertilize and water the more the individual blades of grass will grow and the lawn as a whole will grow faster. This will lead to a fuller thicker lawn but unfortunately more grass cutting. Our prairie environment is designed to create perfect grass growing conditions but there is also a balance between the rate of growth and the rate of decay. By tipping the conditions you upset that balance resulting in too much thatch. I am opposed to people who preach that you must always leave your clippings yet continue to promote excess watering and fertilizing.

Dethatching begins as the poplar trees start to turn grey. If you look at a poplar forest at this time you will see that the trees

will have gone to seed and send out long grey catkins. With thousands upon thousands in the trees it turns all of the poplars grey. This means that the weather conditions are warm enough to start dethatching. Once the grass has fully turned green and the grass is starting to grow then it is too late and it would be better to wait until next year.

There are different methods of dethatching. If you don't rent a dethatching machine then there are two other methods. The first is the old method of using a dethatching rake. It is a special rake with curved blades that bite into the grass. As long as the

grass is still dormant this works really well for cleaning and is an excellent physical work out. The other method is to use a dethatching spring that is attached onto your mower. It comes as a blade with two springs on either side. You change out your regular blade on your mower with the dethatching blade. Set the height on the sidewalk. Try first on a high setting by adjusting the height of the wheels. Walk a pass over your grass. Keep adjusting the height of the wheels until you are able to take out enough thatch without scalping the soil. Please be careful not to stop with the motor running while on the lawn. You will cut a perfect circle right in the middle of the lawn. Not to worry, it will green up in late May but absolutely everyone will know exactly what you did and heckle you.

For yards that face north your yard is usually colder and not quite ready for dethatching in late April. Often you will still have snow on the ground at this time and will have to wait until early May to start your dethatching.

So the basic order for garden clean-up is to first aerate. Wait a week and dethatch. Then blow out your shrub or flower beds on to the lawn. Bag up the debris. Then as a final clean up change your blade back to your regular mowing blade and drop your wheels to the second lowest setting. You will then use your mower as a vacuum and suck up the last of the dead grass, or tree seeds or leaf litter. Then you can add some spring or fall fertilizer and water the sod well.

Spring or fall fertilizer is basically the same thing. If you look on the package, you will see three numbers, example 15-30-15, a common number on a fertilizer box. The first number is for healthy green leaves, the second number is for root growth and flower development and the third number is usually for good health. In the above example, this would be considered a flower or root growth fertilizer because it has a high middle number. I generally recommend using a root fertilizer in the spring to encourage healthy roots. For grass you will only use this once in the spring and maybe once in the fall. Never continue to use a root fertilizer on grass during the summer unless there has been some kind of root damage.

If your sod is patchy or you have animal damage you may want to over-seed. This will help the grass thicken up. You will spread seed at a rate of 0.7 – 1.6 kg/100 square metres. You will need to water for a solid hour and you will have to ensure that you lightly water for the next 14 – 21 days until your new little seedlings can get established.

Another name for over-seeding is top dressing when mixed with soil. This can be done regularly in the spring. The primary purpose of top dressing is to reduce thatch and fix depressions in the soil. You will need to spread soil mixed with grass seed. It is important to choose soil that is the same as your present soil otherwise you will have layering issues in the future. Top dressing by far, is better when applied after dethatching as it adds a layer of microbes directly on top of the thatch. The soil layer should be spread thin over the sod. It is raked and rolled and then watered in. The grass should never be buried under the soil. This is probably the best way to fill in depressions in the lawn, or dead dog patch areas.

Extra jobs for this week are to clean out scummy ponds or

streams in your water feature as the summer birds, such as the robins, are starting to come back and fly north.

A final fun job is to beat the junipers. Take the back end of the rake and brush the evergreens to freshen them up. The rake will knock off old dead leaves and make the junipers look perky.

Cloches

Once gardening has become your life's passion then you will start pushing your zone boundaries. The prairies are primarily between zone 2 in the north to zone 3 throughout. We have incredibly cold and long winters and fairly intense summers. We can grow amazingly colourful gardens, and we have a rich, abundant, and a varied number of perennials and shrubs to choose from, that are all perfectly hardy. Regardless though, we do tend to look longingly at the west coast or central Canada

and their flashy tender perennials. And if you are like me, you run out as soon as you can and buy them. The problem is that if you can get them through the winter with covering they may take so long to start growing that our zone 3 plants will easily out compete them. To get your Zone 4's to grow faster ("push" them) you can use a cloche. A cloche is a plastic or glass dome that increases the temperature around the plant. As long as it has an air vent at

the top to let excess heat escape you can easily push forward a perennial two weeks so that it matches the growth rate of your other more hardy perennials.

As an experiment, I used furniture packing celophane, (or Suran Wrap) and wrapped my grapes. We got amazing growth that year because the grapes had completely leafed out in May. The following year, I did nothing, and the grapes never leafed out until June. I still had a great harvest that year but we worried quite a bit about a fall frost.

As a side note, by this time the Dandelions, Foxtail, and quack grass are all up and ready to be weeded. Details about weeding are on Page 87.

Additional Reading Material:

Williamson, Don (2005). *Lawns for Canada Natural and Organic.* Edmonton, Alberta. Lone Pine Publishing.

May

May should be an exciting time of new growth, new life, and new plant varieties. And it is! But there is a tremendous amount of work to accomplish in May. With good organization and planning though you can fit a lot of work in and have time to enjoy the excitement.

May begins with the first leaves of the Mayday tree. Leafing out can start as early as late April or as late as the 7th of May. The overall objective in May is to finish cleaning and get planting. Vegetable garden soil needs to be turned and seeded, perennial gardens need to be enriched with compost or manure and then at the end of May all of the annuals need to be set out and planted. Let's grab our trusty hoe, on your mark, get set, and lets goooo.

Week 1 in May – Final week for clean up

This is the best time to kill invasive weeds that have infected your shrubs. Usually by now, all of the quack grasses are growing and the thistles, e.g. Canada Thistle and Sow Thistle, should just be starting. The great thing, however, is that the shrubs

are still dormant. Consequently, this is a perfect time to spray with Glyphosate the active ingredient in products like Round-up. Glyphosate kills everything that is green. I do

Unfortunately, every year someone decides to spray weeds in their lawn using Round-Up

need to repeat this, Glyphosate kills everything that is green. You cannot spray it on perennials, shrubs, trees or grasses that have green or coloured leaves on them. Only spray chemical on bark with no open buds.

To get rid of nuisance weeds inside your shrubs there is simply no better way. Often with a single spray of herbicide at the base of a shrub you can kill the weeds. Using a quick spray at this time can save an untold number of hours of weeding through the summer. As soon as the shrubs start showing any sign of growth then that is it for spraying for the rest of the season. You will need to go back to picking away with a dandelion digger for the rest of the summer.

Many of the broad spectrum herbicides come in very handy small spray bottles. Please ensure that you wear rubber gloves, pants and a long shirt. It is best to spray in the early morning with no wind between 15 – 25 degrees. Hope for no rain for 12 hours and keep pets off the grass for 4 hours. If you have quack grass or thistle growing inside a perennial, spray your clean rubber glove and gently squeeze the leaves of the quack grass. Don't pull them out. The objective is to put the chemical on the leaves without harming the perennials. If for any reason you even think you might have dabbed your perennial then immediately wash off the leaves. Should you have dandelions growing in peonies or irises and the perennial hasn't woken up yet, then take a clean "Q Tip" and dip it into a small thimble of chemical and dab the leaves of the dandelion.

Something you need to know is that Glyphosate is inactivated by dirt. So everything has to be clean or you are wasting your time.

Also at this time the elm tree seeds should be starting to drop on to the garden. Elm trees and Manitoba Maples can create a vast amount of seed that, in my mind, has close to a 100% germination. The best way to deal with the seed drop is to use a blower and blow the seeds on to the grass and then vacuum them up with a mower. Or use your blower if you have a vacuum function. Truly the best way to deal with seeds is to remove them from the soil surface and prevent them from being worked into the soil.

The soil in vegetable plots can be turned using a spade and compost and manure added. The cold loving vegetables, example, potatoes and sweet peas can be seeded at this time. You can also build cold frames, which are small plastic houses that are used to heat the soil.

Additional Reading Material:

Balzer, Donna, and Steven Biggs (2012). *No Nonsense Vegetable Gardening. Garden Coaches tell all: No Guff, Lots of Fun.* Pittsburgh, PA: St. Lynn's Press. In Canada, known as *No Guff Vegetable Gardening.* 2011 by No Guff Press.

Week 2 in May – Forking season

The flowering of Nanking Cherries marks the beginning of forking season. Forking season has to be one of my most favourite times in the season. When I began gardening eons ago, most people owned hand tools and only a very few people owned a rototiller. I was hired to fork client's vegetable gardens, and later, when I had a job working as a herb gardener for the Devonian Botanic Garden I spent weeks and weeks forking each of the individual beds. Forking is one of the best ways to remove entire root systems of weeds, especially quack grass, and to aerate and incorporate ameliorants. There is no better way to learn about root structure, bugs, soil composition and soil health. Primarily, because you work your way through the soil inch by inch, or centimetre by centimetre depending upon how exact you want to be.

If you are truly and deeply committed to living a chemical free and carbon neutral lifestyle then you can only succeed by picking up the fork and delving deep into the soil. You stab the fork into the soil, pull out a lump, begin breaking up the soil, and pull out the invasive roots. A good soil should be rich in bugs, worms, rot, twigs, leaves, basically, "Life". It should fall apart easily. Too often I see people take the lazy way of using rototillers. Rototillers destroy soil structure, they cut up invasive roots turning a tiny problem into thousands of new problems. Or if the soil is too wet then what was a nice crumbly soil is instantly turned to rock hard cement lumps. I fully understand that if you have an acre lot or a massive vegetable plot then you have no choice. But in today's gardens which are comparatively quite small, rototillers are not necessary and I think take away from the experience of working with nature. If you are really lucky, Mother Nature will reward you with having a cow bird land on your back while you work. ☺

If your soil is already clean of weeds, you can start straight into adding ameliorants to the garden. I recommend calculating the addition of one inch of peat moss or compost to the soil. Add manure (usually just enough to cover the soil surface). I haven't actually found any difference between the different types of manures but if you want to get gardeners all riled up just disparage them about their choice in poo. The last ameliorant you will need is a tub of bone meal with added fertilizer. (Just a note: Bone Meal takes a couple of years to break down and therefore, acts as a slow release fertilizer for the following year.) You could also substitute sea soil or blood meal. The point is to add some extra slow release nutrients. In the event that you have very hard soil, the usual recommendation is to add course sand. I prefer adding another inch of peat moss (coir, coconut fibre, coffee grounds, etc) or perlite. I rarely recommend sand because people may inadvertently buy too fine of a sand and that only exacerbates the problem. The following year, depending on the soil's clay content, the soil can become even harder than when you started.

For those of you who might be considering entering a garden competition, giving tours, or having large parties or home weddings during the summer, I would consider mixing grass fertilizer into your perennial or shrub beds. Do this only once in the spring. The reason is that the nitrogen in the soil is water-soluble and is at low levels at this time of the year. By adding the extra amount in the spring, you give the plants a good shot in the arm by increasing their leaf production. This boosts the size of the plants and makes for a much more full looking garden. Don't do it after May 21ˢᵗ, though, as you may delay flower development and throw off your timing. It would be horrible to have a 500 person garden tour and not have flowers to show them.

Last note, for yards that are well established and so packed with plants that you don't have enough space for your fork in between the plants, you can put the amendments on the soil surface and leave them to work in on their own. This is called

No Till gardening. Or you can mix them in with a four- pronged cultivator, of which there are now many different brands.

In university, I spent years studying soil learning all about particle ratios, horizons, and on and on. I lost count how often I fell asleep in the back of the class. But

Turn soil to aerate. Mix in peat moss and manure

over the years, I learned a most important lesson: you cannot have a healthy garden without having healthy soil. A healthy garden soil is composed of visible amounts of organic matter, oxygen, i.e., open airy soil, and nutrients.

Golly gosh I am good at pontificating, eh?

Dividing your perennials is another job that can be done in combination with forking. This is covered in more detail in September but now is a great time because you can see the spaces and the plants will have the season to grow.

If you have an irrigation system this is usually a safe time to turn it on or have the irrigation company come in for you. If not, then the big oscillating garden sprinkler will do. The objective is to provide 1" (2.5cm) of water, including rain, per week. Also you want to water for longer periods so that you get a deep watering. Stop once the water starts flowing down the street. If you find you are a forgetful gardener then there are water timers available in any hardware store that will shut off the water after a certain amount of time or after a particular amount of volume has been used.

This is generally also when I stop feeding the birds. Even though they make such an incredible mess through the winter, I love listening to them. It isn't a good idea to build dependency during the summer. I start feeding again at the end of October.

Mid-May is also when I turn off the lighting systems and drain the hot tub. If you are further south it may stay darker later but up where I live the sun is still up into the very late evening which makes a lighting system redundant.

Once the garden has been cleaned up and the soil turned and amended then you can start planting shrubs. For perennials, annuals that you have bought early, or tropicals that you might want to use in pots outside, you will need to harden them off first. For about a week you will need to put them in the semi-shade so that they don't get sunburned. At night, they will have to be covered with blankets to keep them warm. (Tropicals will

have to come inside at night.) After the week long exposure to being outside, and once the temperatures consistently stay above

zero, the plants can be left uncovered but keep the blankets handy. If snow is in the forecast, then bring them all inside for the night. I never forgot the story of my uncle. He bought a new house and being so proud he wanted to have a fantastic garden. After spending quite a few hundred dollars on annuals and roses freshly delivered from Vancouver he planted them on Mother's Day. Two days later it snowed and killed everything. And sadly that was the last time he planted a garden.

Week 3 in May – Fertilizing Schedule

Fertilizing is a giant source of argument among gardeners into which I am not going to weigh into. You don't have to fertilize if you use compost in the garden. Adding manure to the garden IS fertilizing, just a slow release form of it. The garden, in order to do well, needs to be fertilized at least once in the season and the best time is in mid-May. Even in nature, I am sure that Mother Nature sent an animal or two at least once to "water-in" or fertilize each of her plants. For the average homeowner, summer is short and most homeowners want the garden to look good and for plants to grow quickly. Fertilizing is the best way to do that. Whether you choose an organic fertilizer or a high-end inorganic type, or you choose granular or liquid, all of them will help the garden grow lush and quickly.

A caveat on over-fertilizing is that plants become tender, breaking easily, or plants become juicy and attractive to insects. A smaller plant is healthier and lower maintenance. The following list is of fertilizing dates is for good health.

Fertilizing begins on the fifteenth of each month:

For grass, fertilize on:

May 15

June 15

July 15

August 15

For Perennials and shrubs, fertilize on:

May 15

June 15

July 15

And for trees fertilize on:

May 15

June 15

For annuals, fertilize every two weeks, although it is better to do a half concentration and fertilize every week. In greenhouses, they use a low dose concentration and fertilize every day. This is one of the reasons why plants grow so quickly in the garden centres.

Understanding Fertilizers

The primary nutrients are N – nitrogen, P – phosphorus, K – potassium. The proper ratio for grass is 3:1:2 e.g. 21 – 7 – 14

To put this in human terms - Nitrogen, Phosphorus, and Potassium are basically like our Carbohydrates, Proteins, and Fats. They are primary building blocks to building our bodies. The big difference is that plants can make their own food but they can't create their own nutrients. Those nutrients have to come from the soil or air. Also, same as for humans, we can be quite fine with a steak and potato diet but we won't be healthy. We need all the other small vitamins and nutrients like iron, and calcium. So too do plants. They need a whole host of other micronutrients that allow the plant to fight off disease, grow strong, and even to incorporate some of the macronutrients NPK.

Subsequently, when shopping for fertilizers make sure you purchase ones that specifically state that they have additional micronutrients incorporated, whether they are sold as

Figure 1Nitrogen deficiency symptoms - yellow with green veins

organic or not.

As well, read the package for application rates, which are usually a certain amount of kilograms per area. Over or underfeeding one or more of the primary nutrients will result in uneven growth between the top and bottom parts of the plant. There must be a balance between shoot and root growth.

Nitrogen (Used for the leaves)

This is the most mobile of the nutrients and leaches easily through the soil column as you water. You will need to apply nitrogen regularly through the season. Nitrogen affects shoot growth rate and also the colour of the leaves. If nitrogen increases too much (you add just a bit too much nitrogen or too high a concentration on the grass), roots will not be able to keep up and will shut down. If nitrogen continues to increase, the roots will burn. Roots are essential for water and nutrient uptake, and therefore, if the

Dog urine Spots

roots are killed, the rest of the grass will die. A perfect example of that is dog urine. The exact spot where she urinated will die, but there will be a ring of deep green grass around the spot where the concentration was diluted enough for perfect growth. Once the roots and tops are dead the grass is dead. You will have to re-seed and start again.

The correct colour for sod is a dark blue green. A pale greenish yellow colour means that there is a deficiency in nitrogen.

As you continue to add more nitrogen the grass becomes more susceptible to drought, heat stress, and reduced winter hardiness.

The recommended amount is .25 - .75 kg N/100 square metres per growing season. As an example a 10 kg bag of 21-7-14 has 21% Nitrogen in it. 0.21 X 10 kg = 2.1 kg of Nitrogen in the bag. Generally, it is recommended to spread 1 kg N/ season. Let's assume the front is about 1000 square feet (93 square metres). In this example, you can spread a little less than half in the front and the rest in the back throughout the season (not all at once though).

Phosphorus (Used for the Roots)

Phosphorus is very immobile as it becomes locked up in the soil and not accessible to the plant. A soil analysis may show adequate phosphorus levels but the plant may still show purple colouring deficiency symptoms. Here it is important to note that soil microbes are important in converting the phosphorus into a usable form for the plant. Encouraging a rich microbial life in the soil will help the plants to acquire nutrients.

"Phosphorus is vital in the seedling stage. It encourages root growth and development which results in quicker establishment and maturing of the plant." (McKernan, 1994) Phosphorus affects all reproduction and recuperation methods. It is rare to have phosphorus burning as it immediately binds with the soil.

The most common method of application is using a liquid form of the fertilizer usually in the ratio of 15-30-15. And is the best formulation for flower growth.

Potassium (Used for Hardiness)

Turf grasses require large amounts of potassium while young and actively growing. As potassium increases, grass is able to hold water longer and absorbs water more efficiently. This helps the grasses to be more resistant to drought, temperature fluctuations, and also resistance to diseases.

Natural Growth Cycle

The optimum growing temperature for grass is 10 degrees to 18 degrees. The natural growth cycle is to have high growth from May to June and then drop off as temperatures increase beyond 18 degrees. As the temperatures drop there is a small growth spurt in early fall.

Consequently, you need more phosphorus and potassium during slow growth periods and fall. You should have nitrogen available during active growing periods.

You will note in my recommendations that I like a higher middle number fertilizer only once in the early spring and then again in the fall. But you need to use a high first number fertilizer through the season. As long as you fertilize on May 15 and June 15 you should be good for the season. As an experiment, I only fertilized once on May 15. By early October of that year, my grass was yellow and I was getting comments from the neighbours that something looked wrong with my grass.

Mowing Heights

As I am sure you are learning slowly with each turn of the page, for every action there is a reaction. There is an optimal amount of gardening that is perfect for nature but not necessarily for the eye of men. Unfortunately, we like to push a certain look beyond what Nature thinks is optimal and we must deal with the push back from Nature. Even on mowing heights, there are consequences.

"2" cut for a 1 week mow

Most of the grass used in North America is a combination of Kentucky Blue and Creeping Red Fescue. These two types of lawn grass prefer to be cut at 1" to 2" (2.5 cm – 5 cm). At this height the grass is most competitive with other more invasive grasses. Turf that is mowed too short is in a constant state of stress; consequently, making the turf less competitive against weeds. (You will notice that dandelions keep invading the lawn much more frequently.)

As mowing height decreases, the grass blade decreases in size, becoming narrower and thinner. There is a decrease in root and rhizome activity. A note on rhizomes, they are the structure that is just at ground level and creeps along the ground, giving rise to more grass. The plant will increase the shoot growth and stop root production. The grass loses its recuperative ability and weeds eventually become established. If you prefer grass less than one inch, you need to switch to a bent grass.

As mowing height increases the grass increases shoot production resulting in a thicker lawn and increase chlorophyll resulting in a deeper green colour. Often you will see the recommendation of 2 ½" – 2 ¾" (6 cm – 7 cm) for easier maintenance.

To keep the lawn looking its best you can manipulate the lawn by cutting higher in spring and fall and lower in summer. With increased fertilizing and watering, you will increase the rate of growth. Always follow the 30% rule, meaning if you go away on vacation for a couple of weeks and forget to have the grass cut, don't cut the long grass in one shot. Cut it a little bit shorter every third day until you are back to your normal growth height. Golf greens will cut the grass at 1/4" (6mm) resulting in daily mowing.

Kentucky Blue and Red Fescue should be cut at 1 ½" – 2" (3.5 cm – 5cm) thus mowed at 4 – 8 day intervals. If you cut higher then you will need to mow less. Often if you are going on holidays, it is a good idea to let the grass grow taller. Or if the lawn in neglected it is best to leave the grass longer as it can better sustain itself in a healthy state. Keeping the grass at 4" (10cm) will mean that you only need to cut the grass every 2 weeks and keeping the grass at 6" (15cm) height will give you a 4 week interval. So why isn't everyone cutting the grass only once a month? Because it is ugly. These taller heights are only used for acreages or commercial properties.

Remember way back when we were discussing thatch build up. The more frequently you cut the grass the less thatch you will build up. If the grass clippings are smaller you will not have to remove them. Just remember as a general rule: our climate doesn't allow for fast enough degradation of the clippings if you are fertilizing and watering. So after August 15 (first day of fall) and absolutely by September 15 pick up the clippings, otherwise you will begin to get thatch build up.

Still on that note for general mowing practice: keep your blades sharp. Whether you are using a man powered cylinder mower or gas powered push mower sharp blades are hugely important to a good looking lawn. Never mow when the grass is wet. It binds up in the mower but more importantly it shreds the ends of the blades and if you are leaving the clippings on the lawn, the clippings will bind up into a ball and will need to be hand raked.

On the opposite end, don't mow the grass if the weather is super dry and hot and the grass is going dormant. Often people don't water their grass but they still have a mowing company come in and mow. What happens is the grass becomes very susceptible to injury if you walk on it. The weight of the wheels will injure the crowns of the grass in long straight rows. It will look like your lawn mower wheels were soaking in Round-Up

and you decided to mow the grass. Even after the rains come back those wheel rows will remain for some time.

Always change directions each week when mowing, especially on new

If clients were having a party I would create intricate patterns

lawns; otherwise, within two years you will have deep wheel grooves impressed in the lawn. Usually I mow north-south one week, then east-west, and finally diagonally. If I am in a creative mood and bored I will mow in a free form following the contours of the bed or create beautiful circles.

To get the soccer field or baseball diamond groomed look you need a cylinder mower or reel mower with a roller on the back end. A cylinder mower will cut the grass perfectly leaving no dead bits on the end of each blade and you get a perfect green lawn.

Additional Reading Material:

McKernan, Dennis (1994). *Great Plains Turfgrass Manual*. Olds, Alberta: Life Works

Week 4 in May– Annual plantings & pine candle snapping

For annual plantings, there are literally thousands of books on annuals, colour arranging, and use in containers. For this book, I am suggesting that the bulk of your planting be done at this time.

You can start your containers in mid-May and then harden them off by bringing them in and out of the house. For larger containers I would recommend that they be planted at this time. Over the years, I have tried pushing my luck. Sometimes I am rewarded with sunshine and warmth and other times I am blessed with frost and snow to keep me humble.

There are a couple of things to remember when working with annuals. If you are dealing with new introductions, they have been bred to work hand in hand with fertilizing. They are voracious eaters and the only way that you will be able to get your plants looking like they do in the catalogue picture is to fertilize. For my flowerbeds, I use a lot of organic matter in the soil and extra manure, plus I use a liquid fertilizer every two weeks. For pots, you should be using a soilless mix (a potting mix). No garden soil. Garden soil expands and contracts during the winter and can crack your ceramic pots. Because there is no soil you absolutely need to add fertilizer to keep the plants looking full and healthy. My preference is to use a diluted annual fertilizer solution every week.

Annuals are an important must for any garden. They add colour and variety to the look of the garden and bring continual change, which breeds excitement and anticipation for the coming summer.

Since March we have been slowly moving from putzing around the yard to full all out run in May. So not only are you fighting it out in the greenhouses to get the best annuals right now, but the grass is now waking up. I call this time the "push". This is a term that I invented. The soil temperature has warmed up enough that the bacteria in the soil has become active. They start breaking down the organic matter in the soil and releasing the nutrients to the grass. The grass all of a sudden explodes in growth. If you are being more organic, this is the time to apply organic fertilizers to the grass as the bacteria can now work in combination to help the root systems of the grass. It is quite common to have to mow twice this week. The best organic fertilizer that I have found is corn gluten. It slowly breaks down releasing fertilizer throughout the season and it has a seedling inhibiting quality as well. It helps in preventing weeds, such as dandelion, from germinating. There are a couple of negatives though. If you are trying to over-seed your lawn then the corn gluten will prevent the grass from germinating as the gluten cannot distinguish a good seedling from a bad one. Also if you have pets, corn gluten is pure candy. I find that the corn gluten is quite large and it takes about a week to work its way deeper into the lawn. In that time, your dog will just salivate and cry out to go play on the lawn. But all he wants to do is roll around in a bed filled with candy and lick gleefully to his heart's content. My dog had eaten a lot of corn gluten when he was a

puppy and didn't seem to have any ill effects, but I would recommend prevention.

Pine candles are also extending right now and you only have the next two weeks to break the candles.

The proper way to trim pines, example Mugo Pine, is not to hedge them in July like you would do with other shrubs but rather to break the candles now.

You will see a thin little finger beginning to extend from the top of the pine and this finger represents the entire growth for the year. If you break the candle in half you will reduce the growth of the pine by half for the year. If you don't want any growth for the year then you would break the candle off completely.

The mugo pine here has been sheared and you can see the needles have died and turned brown.

Unfortunately, Nature does like to throw a little curve ball from time to time. If you live near the edge of the city, near a ravine, or on an acreage you will have to contend with poplar fuzz. The seeds look like snow and blanket the flowerbeds. It feels like a movie dream sequence, necessitating grabbing a glass of wine and sitting outside under a gazebo and watching the snow fall.

It really is beautiful to watch. However, when all that "snow" stops falling it will need to be picked up. If you have a vacuum attachment it is pretty easy to suck them up, or the seeds can be blown on to the grass and picked up with a mower. The crazy thing is that if it rains, those seeds are incredibly viable and you will get amazing germination in no time at all. The best tool I found that gets rid of these little seedlings is a soil scraper.

Additional Reading Material:

Peters, Laura, Alison Beck, and Don Williamson (2007). *Container Gardening for Canada.* Edmonton, Alberta: Lone Pine Publishing.

Sproule, Rob (2010). *New Annuals for Canada.* Edmonton, Alberta: Lone Pine Publishing.

Williams, Sara, & Hugh Skinner (2011). *Gardening, Naturally. A chemical-free handbook for the Prairies.* Regina, Saskatchewan: Coteau Books

June

April and May are exhausting. I liken it to waking up in the morning, dragging the spouse out of bed, getting your 6 kids up, washed, and fed. Checking in on the spouse, finding your keys, scraping the windshield, and actually making it to work on time. Oh yah, did you let the dog back in the house before you left?

June, July and August are the months that we on the prairies can truly enjoy the garden and the act of gardening. People love gardening because they can let their mind wonder mindlessly as they pull out weeds and water the pots. Time floats by and before you know it the day is gone. To many, this is therapy after a long week in the office. But I would like you to try something a little different for at least half an hour each week. Your mind has an incredible ability to float mindlessly back and forth from the past to the future. You think about your future holidays, or dinner tonight, or how you composed an email last week. So often, our mind isn't present to what we are doing right now. Our hands move on their own while we think about what our kid's soccer schedule is this month. At least once a week for a half hour, be mindful of the now. Feel the soil between your fingers, smell the aroma, hear the tools push through the soil, and see the roots, bugs, and soil composition. Lift your head and feel the sun on your face. Just sit there for a moment and feel that sensation. When you hear the birds, stand there, close your eyes, and listen to them. As you are dead heading the finished flowers, listen to the scissors cut the stem and feel the sensation of the flowers in your hands. If your mind fights back and wants to think about what is on TV tonight, don't scold it, gently guide your mind back to feeling the wood of your dandelion digger. Let your hands rule the body for a bit. Feel and experience your surroundings. At the end of the summer, when you look back, those will be the memories that you will have. Being present, being in the moment. Some of my great memories are of when a robin sat on a rock waiting, and then swooping in to score a worm while I was forking the soil; or when my dog and I stared into the sky as thousands upon thousands of Canada geese flew overhead. Even a small moment when 6 white butterflies hovered about in the garden like a group of pixie faeries having a conversation. There is a shocking amount of beauty out there when you feel, hear, see, and taste the garden with mindful awareness.

Week 1 in June – Composting and Weeding

I believe in the incredible benefits of composting and have seen those benefits, but truth be told, I am horrible when it comes to composting. Compost is created by the breakdown of plant material into a very basic form which is then incorporated back into the soil. It is formed by mixing fresh "green" material (fresh cut perennials or lawn clippings) with dry "brown" material (leaves or stems) and letting that heat up over the course of the summer. The bacteria, combined with heat and oxygen, eats away at the plant material turning it into a rich, nutritious soil amendment.

There are many different ways of creating compost. You can throw it into a pit and let it rot slowly, or put it into inexpensive wooden containers or incredibly expensive plastic styles. I have tried all kinds of different styles, even trying a bucket full of worms but nothing really worked for me. I finally found a small plug in style machine that heats, turns, and oxygenates all by itself. Yes, I truly am that lazy but I love my little electric composter. The main issue with compost is the belief that it smells. And, it does. The trick is to get the right ratio between the greens and the browns, make sure you have good heat build-up, and that you turn the mix periodically to add in oxygen. The result is an incredibly nutritious amendment for the soil.

There are many courses and books available. Once you are hooked, it is a lot of fun to discover all of the different kinds of things that you can compost.

Weeding

I read a wonderful Zen book recently that glorified not the attainment of one's goal but the path towards those goals. It went on about how we need to take the time to enjoy the journey and as goals come and go, the enjoyment of the journey remains. I am positive this man never spent a day weeding in the garden. Whether you are puttering, muttering, or aching, weeding, like it or not, is your path to enlightenment.

Everyone has their own way of weeding, but your primary method of weeding will be to use cultural methods of pulling out weeds by the root or cutting them off at the root. You don't always have to collect the weeds. If they are small you can just leave them on the soil surface to dry up in the sun. As much as possible, try to weed regularly so that weeds are kept small. If the weeds get too big they will have to be removed and preferably thrown away. I don't compost larger weeds that may go to seed.

When I started my gardening business, I needed to get rid of weeds quickly and economically, otherwise clients wouldn't continue hiring me. I used a combination of both chemical and cultural methods. My main tactic is to use chemicals early in May to get rid of perennial and highly invasive weeds before the rest of the garden starts growing. Once the perennials and shrubs are growing then I switch to hand work for the rest of the summer. You don't have to use herbicide but careful, thoughtful application makes gardening much easier to manage.

Pictures of the tools I like using in the garden:

Pruning Saw
Hedger
Dandelion digger/knife
Hand Rake
Perennial Spade
3 Pronged Cultivator
Soil Scraper

4 Pronged Cultivator
Variety of Arrow Hoe
3 pronged Cultivator
Oscillating Stirrup Hoe

Hand
Pruner,
Extendable
Pruner,
Various
Dandelion
Diggers,
Stirrup Hoe,
Soil Scraper,
3 pronged
Cultivator

Here is the quickest way that I have found to get rid of weeds:

Quack grass – Usually imported with infected soil, I use glyphosate (e.g. Round-Up) in late April, or I fork out the roots in mid-May. If it has infested a plant, e.g. Daylilies, I let it grow. In mid to late June, the daughters will venture out and away from the daylily but will be still attached to the mother. I then spray the daughters. The daughters will carry the chemical to the mother plant that lives inside the perennial and destroys the root.

If the grass is in a carpet juniper, then you let the grass grow taller than the juniper. Spray a rubber glove and lightly squeeze the grass blades without pulling on them. Both of these methods will take most of the summer but will remove it.

Culturally: use a fork two days after rain or watering. The soil will be soft and generally falls away from the web of white roots. If the roots are intertwined in a perennial you will have to pull the entire plant out, tweeze out the quack grass and then replant. Be as careful as possible to not break the roots.

Canada thistle and Sow thistle - are just evil and have deep

root systems. Often the mother plant may live in someone else's yard. Here you need to use a combination of glyphosate and 2-4D (e.g. Round-Up and Killex). Spray glyphosate in early May and then three days later spray with 2-4D. Not later, otherwise the plant will start to shut down and won't accept the 2-4D. If you have a thistle growing inside a shrub or perennial it will be difficult to spray it. You will have to let it grow so that you have more green leaves and then brush it with a paintbrush dipped into a cup of glyphosate or 2-4D.

Culturally, it is very difficult to remove by hand. The best method that I found is to fork down around 16 inches. You are looking for a horizontal root that gives rise to all of the vertical roots. If it is a new plant you can hoe it consistently and slowly starve it out.

Dandelion - Don't allow the lawn to dry out and go dormant, as dandelion seed comes in by air and succeeds when there is

no competition. In the grass, use a hand spray and spray the Dandelions individually with 2-4D. (You can buy premade mixes that come in handy sized small spray bottles.) REMEMBER, don't use Round-Up on your lawn, Round-Up or the active ingredient in it, glyphosate, kills everything green.) I am not a fan of spraying grass that doesn't have any dandelions in it. It is wasteful and certainly not environmental. In the garden, if the weed is very small use a hoe and let it die in the sun. Once the leaves are longer than your pinky finger you will have to use a dandelion digger and remove the entire root. Cutting the tops off will do nothing. If it is growing inside a perennial, I try to pull the tops off to starve it somewhat, but basically, I wait until the first week in May and paint brush it with glyphosate.

Foxtail – This is an air borne weed that is quite pretty and is often purposefully left to grow. The problem appears next year

when you have literally thousands of seedlings everywhere. As it is an annual weed you don't need chemicals, but you will need a good hoe as the fibrous roots are quite strong.

Annual weeds – These are weeds that start from seed, grow, flower, and reseed all in one season. Main examples are Stinkweed, lamb's quarter, nettle, etc. Don't use chemicals. Hand tools like a hoe, soil scrapper, or dandelion digger are better. You don't have to

remove them. I usually hoe them on a sunny day or a day with a good breeze and then just leave them on the soil to dry up. Don't hoe if the soil is wet or if there is going to be rain. These weeds will just re-root and carry on as if nothing happened.

Additional Reading Material:

Ondra, Nancy J. (1998). *Soil and Composting. The complete guide to building healthy, fertile soil.* New York, NY: Houghton Mifflin Company.

Week 2 in June – Spring Flowering Shrub Trimming & Staking

Trimming

Two types of trees that could not be pruned until this week are the Birch and the Maples. They have such a high sap flow pressure that if you cut them in spring they bleed non-stop for weeks. This doesn't kill them but makes a huge mess and starts a vicious pest cycle. The sap is liquid sugar that then attracts the aphids. The aphids excrete sweet honeydew that attracts ants to protect them and the ants then harvest the honeydew. Leftover honeydew then grows black fungus that stains sidewalks and tree bark.

Once the trees have fully leafed out then it is safe to prune them. Back when I was in my 20s, the old guys at that time said not to prune until July. But I have found because of climate

change plants are earlier than they used to be and June is safe enough.

Spring flowering shrubs are all shrubs that flower before June 21. These include your Forsythia, *Prunus* (Nankings,

White flowering spirea

sandscherry, etc), white flowering spirea and lilacs.

In early April, we did thinning. That is where you remove whole branches to air out the shrubs allowing them to breathe, and shape them. But if you want to head them back or pinch them so that they thicken up, then the

Wedgewood blue Lilac

perfect time to trim them would be within two weeks of them

finishing to flower. They absolutely must be trimmed before June 21. After this they set their buds for next year.

I have heard so many stories of people who have never had a lilac bloom because they treat their shrubs like other shrubs and trim them in the fall or in March. What they are doing is cutting off all of the flowers. Yes, your plant will do incredibly well; it will be thick and healthy but if you cut off their flowering buds then you will not have flowers.

Sometimes plants just get overgrown and need to be deeply cut back and re-invigorated. The best time to do that is late March or early April, but just remember you will get no flowers for the current year.

Perennial Staking

Beginning when the French lilacs start blooming, a task this week, before the perennials get too big, is to stake them. This means, to create a little cage so that the plants don't get so tall that they then flop over and "donut." So often you see this with peonies whose flowers are just so heavy that the plant bends over, and the flowers point to the ground.

There are all kinds of cages: tomato cages, peony cages, and delphinium wires. But rebar or bamboo sticks and garden jute twine work just as well. A note, though, if you are entering a

Peonies have a large heavy flower that needs support

garden competition in July your staking must be invisible and therefore needs to be ¾ the height of the plant. In this way, the judges will only see the plant and not the stakes propping it up.

In the case of tall perennials like Delphiniums or Rudbeckias, you will often have to string them up against a fence to keep them from breaking in the wind.

Tree Weeds

Right about now tree seedlings: Green Ash, Caragana, Elm, and Manitoba Maple, should be popping up in the garden. In early May, I recommend blowing the seeds that fell from the trees into the grass or into a corner and pick them up. In general, if you are weeding and cultivating regularly you don't  get tree seedlings growing in the flowerbeds as they are easy to kill by hand, but what usually happens is the tree seeds fall inside the shrubs. They then start to grow and are camouflaged by the shrub and within two years you have a tree that is the size of the shrub. Usually in the third year the tree is now taller than the shrub and that is when you finally notice it. Unfortunately, by this point you will have a massive root system, just cutting it down won't solve the problem. You will have to be extremely careful and use herbicide on the tree leaves without dropping anything on to the shrub below. The tree will live through the first couple of applications. But by the end of August, you will have killed it. Only once all the leaves are brown can you then go and remove the main stem.

An odd job that isn't gardening *per se* is sealing your pavers in your patio or your sidewalk and driveway. I mention this because I believe that enjoying time with family, or by yourself sitting on the patio, is one of the big points of gardening. Why have a gorgeous garden if you or your family aren't going to sit out on the patio and gaze loving at your garden? Patio pavers have come an incredible distance from the old pink zigzag pavers of long ago. They have interesting colours and textures now as well. In order to preserve the paver itself, but also to enhance its colours, sealing your pavers is absolutely rewarding.

Also if you have an aggregate driveway or coloured concrete you do need to seal every other year or the driveway  will slowly start to deteriorate. There is a reason why I recommend sealing in June though. A dangerous trait about sealing is that it makes the surface slippery in winter. Absolutely, do not seal in fall. The sealant will make your sidewalks like pure ice in winter. But by sealing in June, the sealant has time to wear down a little and will be safer once the snow falls. Paver sealant is sold at larger landscape supply houses and in the paint department at most hardware stores.

Week 3 & 4 in June – Disease and Pests

As I am sure you have guessed so far, I am a giant proponent of cleanliness in the garden. Primarily, for a reason that is just odd. Way back in my third year of university I ran out of money, as many kids do, and had to have a full time job as well as doing a full course load. The problem was that all of my pest and disease courses were in that year. I got through the year but without much sleep, or food for that matter, and I didn't truly learn anything. So starting my own business I, for many years, felt quite inept in identifying and treating problems. The best recourse though was to be clean. Like the saying from an old TV commercial from when I was a kid, "Clean, Yes. Germs, No."

Remove dead debris. Either incorporate it into the soil, compost it, or if it is infected, throw it away. Turn the soil in late October, as many pests lay eggs in the soil to over winter and come back the following year. Keep air circulation both within a plant and amongst plants. Therefore, good pruning practices are a must. Keep your plants healthy and well watered. Just a side note, don't let your plants get fat. Over feeding them makes them big, week stemmed, and juicy. You end up with more problems. Practice prevention: using dormant oil at the end of April on shrubs or trees to prevent insects from hatching, using netting on vegetables to prevent butterflies and moths from laying eggs, or using protective wraps around tree stems. The hard truth: if you want a good garden you must be a good gardener.

There are hundreds of diseases and pests out there but there are just a few that are common to everyone's garden across the prairies. I definitely would recommend doing online searches and purchasing a few books.

Ants

Ants strangely are reviled as the greatest scourge to gardener-kind, but actually don't cause that much damage. They injure plants only when they are burrowing through the soil, or creating their cone shaped towers in the middle of your lawn. They do a little of their own agriculture, as well, as they tend aphid flocks. They protect aphids, mealybugs, and scale so that they can collect their droppings called honeydew. This honeydew is brought back to the nests to feed their little grubs. Isn't that just precious. Also, they will bite you really hard and freak you right out when they swarm up your leg.

There are all kinds of remedies - from boiling water to the absolute worst, using Borax and icing sugar. I would recommend using ant traps or ant powder and just encourage the ants to move over to the neighbour's yard by continually harassing the colony.

Aphids

Aphids affect a whole host of plant material but primarily on Roses, Lupines, and Ninebark.

They can be a number of colours but usually yellow, green, or a blueish black. They are primarily identified by having two cornicles or horns on their back ends. They suck the sap from the leaves and stems and they multiply at an unbelievable rate. During the summer, they are all female and in the garden world, everyone will tell you that they are born pregnant. They over winter as eggs in the bark of trees, or in the soil near perennials.

For perennials, I have noticed that they are worse if you over feed and make the plants too juicy and weak. The best remedy is to run your fingers along the stems and squish them. Wash the stems every two or three days with water or spray them with an insecticidal soap or garlic spray. (Note: if you ever have time during the year to read *The Truth About Garden Remedies* by Jeff Gillman, it is a must. The author is a professor and made it his mission to scientifically test out homemade remedies to see which ones worked and which ones were useless. Incredibly interesting.)

For shrubs, use the same remedy as above, but in late April spray the stems with dormant oil before the shrubs leaf out. The dormant oil smothers the eggs and helps hinder their hatching.

In August, the aphids change and become either winged males or females and fly off together to create new colonies.

Blackspot on Roses

To me Blackspot on roses is a cleanliness issue. It is a fungus
that overwinters
on an infected
stem or on
infected leaves
left on the
ground over
winter. The
black spots
appear on the

leaves and then multiply so badly that the leaf turns yellow and
drops off. If you do nothing the rose could die.

I highly recommend cleaning the roses thoroughly in the fall
and remove all leaves and ensuring that the roses are pruned so
that there is good air movement between branches. In late
April, before the leaves appear, spray with dormant oil, which
can be purchased at any greenhouse. During the summer if you
notice blackspot it is better to spray with a chemical approved
for black spot.

Delphinium Leaf Tier

During the summer in the late evenings, there is a golden brown moth that will fly about your delphiniums and begin laying eggs at the base of your perennials. In the spring, the small green larvae will begin to sew up the upper leaves and once protected inside, begins to eat the developing flower stem. The delphinium itself will continue to grow but you will notice that all of the flowering stems will turn black and you won't get any flowers.

There is a dirty little secret they don't tell you when you signed up for gardening. It is the "ick" factor. There are some pests that you can't just sprinkle with pixie dust and they will magically go away. With delphinium leaf tier you will need to squish them. Because they are sealed up inside their protective leaf blanket you cannot use a contact spray. So you will have to use your fingers and squeeze the leaves until you hear a small quiet pop sound. Think of it as bubble wrap. We do a walk through the garden every morning with coffee to see what is new in bloom. While walking, I make sure I pop at least 10 of them every morning from the middle of May to the middle of

June. (Just a note, I love Delphiniums and have a yard full of them so you won't have to do that many each morning.)

Powdery Mildew

This is a fungus that usually attacks Monarda, Phlox, Roses, Delphinium, and Geranium.

Unfortunately, these are the big flower power perennials in the garden and once one gets it, the fungus can easily skip to the next species and infect more leaves.

It is strange though, that everyone recognizes it as a fungus and would think that it would like moist shady spots, but, in fact, powdery mildew is worse when conditions are dry and your plants are under water stress. The spores are spread by wind; thus, having good air circulation within plants and among plants is a good preventative method. Interestingly, the spores are sensitive to injury from rain droplets so watering your plants well keeps them healthy and inhibits the mildew.

With powdery mildew there are some great homemade remedies but a good fungicide application as soon as you see the mildew is the best defense. If the plant is completely covered with fungus, e.g. with Monarda, Geranium, or Salvia, cut the plant to the ground. It will regrow and put out healthy new growth that often doesn't get re-infected.

Slugs

Nothing more disgusting than slugs. Slugs generally are known for eating your Hosta and Hollyhocks although they do eat a number of different plants.

Slugs prefer dark, moist, cool conditions, which are often on the north facing side of your yard where you would plant shade- loving plants like Hosta.

They feed at night by chewing large irregular holes in the leaves and in the fall will overwinter in the soil and in plant debris.

Keeping the soil clean of debris and turning the soil deeply (which we will talk in depth about in mid-October) are your main defenses. Usually books recommend hand picking them but I find their slimy little bodies wriggle between my fingers and they end up falling on the ground. Slug traps work very well. Keep the beer in the fridge, though, and use a good slug bait. My preference is to use copper netting or diatomaceous earth. As they crawl like zombies towards your perennials they end up slicing their tummies and dying. Sad but necessary.

As a precaution you can also spread some aluminum sulphate around the base of the perennials in spring to treat the eggs as they hatch.

June 21

In the vegetable garden, many of the cold crops are done and need to be pulled up as the light level will cause them to start bolting and going into seed. Usually, at this time you can start seeding another crop, example beets or another variety of

lettuce, etc. (Balzer 2012, *No Nonsense Vegetable Gardening*)

This is the actual first day of summer and also the time to give up on dead things. As all gardeners are filled with hope and mercy, we keep wishing life into dead things. But no matter how much water and fertilizer we give that dead rose, or struggling tomato, it isn't going to magically come back to life. Right about now the greenhouses are usually having full on greenhouse clear outs and this is a good time to rush out and get a deal. Say a prayer, shed a tear as you look at pictures from last year, and think about what might have been. Then yank it out and throw it into the compost. Yeah, Shopping!

Additional Reading Material:

Bradley, Steven (2007). *What's Wrong with my Plants? Expert information at your fingertips.* London, England: Octopus Publishing Group.

Gillman, Jeff (2008). *The Truth about Garden Remedies. What Works, What Doesn't, and Why.* Portland, Oregon: Timber Press.

Nora Bryan, and Ruth Staal (2003). *The Prairie Gardener's Book of Bugs. A guide to Living with Common Garden Insects.* Calgary, Alberta. Fifth House Ltd.

July

July is truly my most treasured time in the garden. There is so much abundance. The flowers are resplendent, the animal and bird watching are great fun, but most importantly there are people. I have long said in my landscape design courses that people get caught up in designing great flower beds, butterfly gardens, or bird sanctuaries but so often forget about the most important component - "Us". I have been to quite a few splendid gardens, filled with spectacular plants yet for people there will be only a small table and four chairs stuck out in the middle of the lawn as an after-thought. People are also an integral part of the garden and so, as gardeners, we have to figure out what kinds of things humans like, so that they will be attracted and stay a while in the garden as well.

I love my garden and would force friends that came to our

house in the summer to sit outside. But that only lasted for a couple of hours as before long everyone would be back inside looking out. Humans like soft padded chairs, light, and heat. They are easily spooked, so mosquitoes and bees are public enemy number one. Water sounds are soothing but the smell of food is the clincher. Heartbreakingly enough, flowers only hold their attention so long. Definitely while shopping in the greenhouses this summer, look at furniture. There are amazing sets out there now with long lasting outdoor fabrics. Candles, lanterns, and lighting systems are very affordable and create a luminous ambiance during the evening. Gazebos with included mosquito netting are available in all the box stores. Electric or propane outdoor heaters are a must. Heaters extend your evening enjoyment but they also extend your season as you can sit outside earlier in the spring and later in the fall. You may be repulsed at the idea of having to attract humans, as most gardeners think of them as being quite destructive, but in doing so you might end up spending even more time outside yourself.

Week 1 in July – Hedging Season Begins

As soon as the Mock oranges finish flowering, hedging season begins. Way back at the beginning of March we learned the rules of pruning. Never cut more than a third, don't prune Birch and Maple until June, plants either grow up or out, spring pruning invigorates, and July pruning slows plants' growth rate. Once our plants reach the height or spread that we want them to be, then we no longer want to prune in late winter or early spring but rather we want to trim in July so that we can maintain them at a certain height. Shearing (more or less the same meaning as hedging or trimming) at this time will cut the plants' energy levels and slow them down. Also, after June 21 most shrubs and trees are done with their major grow spurt so they will hold their shape longer. Usually we follow with another touch up hedging in mid-September.

There are a couple of important rules you need to understand when hedging. One, the prairies, both in Canada and the northern US, are not England. We simply cannot have the perfectly straight up and down hedges that they have. Our hedges must be cut at an angle, i.e. slightly pyramidal, otherwise the hedges will die out at the bottom because they won't get enough sunlight. Any pruning book will have detailed pictures about the correct angle, but suffice it to say, they cannot be perfectly straight.

Also, you must account for how your body moves. When trimming along the sides of your hedge you need to realize that your body seesaws back and forth from left to right. So your hedger will wave in and out as you walk. Paying attention to the movement of the hedger is all-important to being able to cut a clean line. Ensure that you have good body posture. Keep your back straight, shoulder's

relaxed, and knees slightly bent. The hedger itself, whether a machine or shears, must be perfectly level.

When the movie Edward Scissor Hands came out I

was awe struck. When I grew up, I had to create hedges like that, but in the real world, I realized it is a little harder than they make it look in the movies. Being able to see the form before you trim is so important. If you are creating a ball then you must see the ball in your mind's eye first. Then begin trimming from the top down. If you make a mistake, stop. Far too often people start out with a four-foot shrub and then after a series of mistakes and aggressive over corrections they walk out with a one-foot shrub.

Week 2 in July – Getting Ready for Garden Tours

July is when the garden is at its most magnificent. It is also garden tour season. Every city and most towns will have garden tours and some of the larger cities will have garden competitions through their different horticulture societies. I absolutely recommend spending a couple of weekends in July and August supporting your local horticulture society or group and visiting gardens in your community. Talk with the owners and complement them on all of their hard efforts. Eventually, take the plunge and try your hand. The judges often give very good advice on improving your garden and in a couple of years, you just may win. Although, everyone says it's not about the winning … it really is.

Some of the things that judges look for are healthy looking plants. No diseases, or at least they have to look like they are being treated. The plants need to be staked up (your cages should not be visible) and deadheaded. That is, you must remove all spent flowers. The soil needs to be fluffy, *i.e.* freshly cultivated, and free of weeds. I judged for many years and we counted all of the weeds. Any more than 5 was a big error to us.

Also, we looked at other things: do you have noxious or banned weeds or plants, is your composter clean and tidy, are your trees and shrubs trimmed properly, and is your lawn green and free of dandelion.

Depending on what category you are competing in, the judges also look at design, four season plantings, and accent features. People will often compete for three or four years until they finally get a first. And it is incredibly satisfying. I have seen many examples of smaller homes knocking out large homes simply because they are the better gardeners.

If you are not into competition then many people have wedding parties or big summer splashes, where the garden is the venue. I know, "Pride goeth before a fall," but truly when everyone is walking through the garden with a glass of wine in hand adoring how beautiful the garden is, gosh that makes you feel good.

Week 3 & 4 in July – Last Day of Summer

Right about now, I have to compliment you. You have worked incredibly hard up to now and your garden is "GLORIOUSSSS!" Yeah for you! July and August are months

to enjoy the garden. You will have only the very basic of weeding to do because sadly July 15 is the last day of summer.

This day is usually the last day for fertilizing, although you can still fertilize the grass again on August 15. Personally, I don't. By now I have had quite enough of the garden and lying out on the patio in the sun is a true gift.

Even though, the calendar says we are still in the beginning of summer, the light levels are changing noticeably for the plants. This causes them to begin switching over for the coming fall. Since spring, nutrients and water have been flowing upwards into the top of the tree canopy, flowers, and seeds have been formed, and right about now the plants are starting to think about storage. It takes a couple of weeks but the flow of the sap comes to a stop and starts reversing so that by mid-August the nutrients start flowing down and the roots start to find places to store the food for the coming winter.

August

Week 1 in August – Harvesting

Strawberry

Saskatoon

If you have a vegetable garden, you have been harvesting all of the cold crops and have been picking tomatoes for a few weeks, depending on when you did your initial plantings. But now the fruit crops are starting. Usually, the first weekend in August, starts with the raspberry U-Pick farms opening. Then right on the raspberry's heels are the saskatoon, cherries and early apples. I know a lot of people who drive to the Okanagan in BC with empty vehicles to load up on tomatoes and fruit for canning. The stores are stocked up with canning supplies and pickling spices. This is such a great time for children to become

involved in the garden. They can see the fruit, eat it and then learn how to preserve it, freeze it, make jam and then eat some more. For children early exposure to nature can fire up their imaginations, and help develop a keen interest in the world around them.

When I was a kid, we lived up in the high arctic in a tent on the Mackenzie River. I had my own rabbit traps and fishing nets that needed to be checked every morning (at least, I think it was the morning, it was always daylight and I remember never being sure what time it was). After everything was skinned and fish set out for drying we jumped into boats and went off to secret sites on the tundra. There I learned how to identify strawberries, blueberries, and cranberries. When we got back to camp, I then learned all of the amazing things that you could then do with the harvest. That experience had a deep and lasting impact on my life. Well, that and the grizzly attack.

Week 2 in August – An Excellent Time to Kill Things

Just as in growing things, there is also a perfect time to kill things. Let's take an example: you have a 15-year-old lilac that needs to be killed. In March you cut it down because the ground was frozen and it made it easier to remove it, and then spent almost the entire summer spraying it with glyphosate trying to kill it and it just wouldn't die. What went wrong? First of all, the energy from 15 years of growth was sent into the root system during the preceding fall for storage. By cutting it down in March you pruned for invigorated plant growth. Being that there was no longer any tree there the lilac sent up thousands of suckers from every root in the yard. Round-Up, in order to work effectively, needs to work its way down into the root system. But in spring all of the energy is moving from the root system up into the stems and leaves so your chemical is trying to fight against the current. The best time to kill a tree or shrub is in August. The plant is still growing vigorously so you have lots of green leaves that will take the spray. But now you have the actions of the plant to help you. All of the systems in the plant are reversing and the plant is taking sugars deep down into the root system for storage. By spraying now, the chemical can work incredibly effectively in killing the entire plant right when it is most vulnerable. I would spray through August and September and then remove the plant in early October.

Week 3 & 4 in August – First day of Fall & Turning on the Lights

August 15 is the first day of fall. Even though the calendar says it is a month away all of the plants are in full storing mode and you will have already noticed, here and there, the odd yellow leaves in the trees. By mid-September, a number of the perennials will need to be cut back already.

Usually mid-August is when I turn my lighting system back on as it is finally getting dark enough, and early enough for the lights to have an impact.

Also, this is a good time to start up the hot tub, although many people like to start it up during the September long weekend.

You can do one last fertilizing on the lawn but not after this date, as you will encourage week grass going into winter if winter comes early.

On that note, winter is supposed to come nine weeks after the last pink flowering fireweed has flowered in your area.

Limelight Hydrangea as a standard, a stunning late August addition to the garden

September

Over many years of working with people and being outside for the entire summer, I have developed a strange philosophy about September. I believe that over the course of millions of years of evolution our bodies, once re-exposed to the weather, reboot and instinctually know that winter is coming. I know it happens with me and I have seen it with my employees over and over again, but I become voracious. I want to eat, but not only that, at the same time I want to preserve and squirrel away food as well. So a few years ago, I decided to learn how to can fruit from my trees and then make pies for the winter.

This may seem normal to most people but you have to understand my history. I can't cook. I have poisoned myself fairly badly a few times. I have set a fire in the BBQ and melted my house, and even blew up the microwave. Once I thought I would make instant melted chocolate. I misread the instructions so instead of microwaving it for 30 seconds I nuked it for 30 minutes. I actually had to take a hammer and chisel to the bowl and chip out the chocolate. So when I announced that I was going to learn to can all my friends sat dead silent, and then said "Kevin, are you sure that's a good idea? You know you have problems even turning on the stove."

Well, after quite a few years of courses, books, and watching demonstrations, I have finally become reasonably competent at canning and
baking. I truly love making pies now and knowing that everything has come from my garden makes me feel incredibly proud. The problem is, no matter how many pies I make, they never last to December.

Week 1 in September – Dividing Perennials

If you didn't divide your perennials in the spring then the next best time is in September. A good perennial book or some on line sites e.g. Finegardening.com are a good resource for learning when and how to divide perennials. Not all perennials need splitting but many perennials will start to die out in the centre as they age. If this is the case, you will have to dig out the perennial, split it, and amend the soil before replanting.

My preference is to divide in the fall because all of your plants are at maturity and you can see where the spaces in the garden are. There are often holes in your blooming times as well. Sometimes through the summer there will be periods where there is not enough plants in flower. So by dividing the plants that are in bloom at that time you can

develop a more balanced garden. Also, by moving the plants now, the perennials will have two months to set root and make it through their first winter. Make sure that you give the plants a dose of a high middle number fertilizer to promote root growth.

Fall Containers

Over the years, I have learned something interesting about people and their container plantings. In the spring and especially during the summer, people are feverish about maintaining their pots. They are watered, fertilized,  deadheaded, and adored. But by mid-August they get forgotten and are quite dead by mid-September. Should this have happened to you I highly encourage you to pull out the dead plants and replant with a new fall arrangement. The garden centres bring in a whole host of new plants like chrysanthemums, ornamental kale and smaller sunflowers. This brightens up the verandah and uplifts the spirits for the brilliant leaf colours to come. The pots can also be further dressed up with pumpkins for Thanksgiving.

On another note, for garden maintenance, I usually recommend severely reducing the watering of the plants except where needed. The idea is to force your plants to start preparing for winter.

Week 2 in September – Touch up Hedging

Your primary hedging is usually done in July as this is the perfect time to reduce growth rates in your shrubs. But many of the plants will continue to grow and will start to look a bit shabby. Doing a touch up hedging right now will smarten up the shrubs so that they look good throughout the winter. Remember though, that you cannot hedge or prune spring flowering shrubs if you want them to flower next year.

If you are not concerned with the flowers then absolutely you can prune.

Don't however, prune trees. Pruning in September can shake them up a bit and may encourage them to start putting out new growth. Pruning of trees doesn't start again until they have dropped all of their leaves in late October.

Week 3 & 4 in September – Bulbs and First Cut Backs

By now all of the greenhouses, grocery stores, and hardware stores are full of bulbs. I know you are starting to get tired of the garden but bulbs in the spring are incredibly energizing and worth the extra time in planting. You can plant bulbs as late as

the end of October, but the bulbs do need the time to set down roots before they can extend their flowers. Therefore, the later you plant bulbs the later the bulbs will come up in spring. When I first started gardening, I planted my bulbs according to the instructions. I dug a six to eight inch (15cm – 20cm) hole and planted them pointy side up. And somewhere around mid-June they came up. Many of the bulbs now are not as long lived as the original Darwin hybrids so you are better off planting tulips 3"- 4" (7cm – 10cm) down and daffodils 4" (10cm). Ensure you dust them with bulb dust (fungicide) to protect them. I

find that they come up much earlier and I think that they will pick up fertilizer the following year easier and re-flower the next spring. Depending where you buy your bulbs, prepare for about 80% to 90% of them to come up and flower.

For the non-Darwin hybrids you can often get 2 or 3 years out of them before they stop blooming. When that happens most people dig them up and plant new bulbs.

Early Cutbacks

Ferns

Generally, the nights are starting to get cool and often there is a touch of frost in the mornings. This will cause the ferns, lilies, and Hostas to turn yellow.

Lilies

Usually, I start cutting back these perennials as soon as they completely turn yellow. It reduces the amount of work that will need to be done later in October.

Last note, for some fruit, such as apples and grapes, they will need cold and particularly frost to sweeten up. If your apples are not tasting right, try leaving them later in the season to see if a cold treatment will make them taste better.

October

October is the same as April, in that it is a time for cleaning. But there is one more responsibility and that is protection. You do have to protect your plants physically with wraps to prevent animals from eating your plants through the winter or winter winds from desiccating the flower buds. But we also have to be on guard for pests overwintering in the soil and re-infecting the plants again next year. October is a perfect time to think about prevention.

Week 1 in October – Final Mow and Blowing out Irrigation Lines

By now, your lawn will have completely slowed down. This is usually the garden's final mow. Although don't put away the mower as it is useful for picking up leaves after doing cut backs in mid-October.

If you have an irrigation system, you will need to have your system blown out. Irrigation systems are fairly precise and if water freezes in the lines over winter the ice can severely damage the heads, or worse, crack the main line somewhere in the soil. Most people have the company that installed the system; come back and blow out the lines. If not, then it can be done at home by renting an air compressor. You will find that most equipment rental shops will already be set up to rent a compressor for just this sort of thing. The compressors are heavy so it is best to have a truck or van so that you have enough space to maneuver it.

There is one slight annoyance. At the very end of October, you need to water in the trees and shrubs for the winter. You cannot use your irrigation lines once they have been blown clean so you will have to resort to using the old sprinklers. Therefore, don't put away your garden hoses just yet.

Week 2 in October – Perennial Cutbacks

For some families, Christmas is their biggest celebration, for others maybe an anniversary, but for my family, it is Thanksgiving. Our tradition is that everyone contributes only homemade dishes, preferably with food that you grew or collected. Even now, as I write this, I can practically taste the freshly pulled carrots, potatoes, and beats. Swiss chard rolls, perogies, and homemade breads all steamy out of the oven. And from our outdoor slow cooker an insane melt-off-the-bone turkey or lamb. The entire dinner is held outside on the patio. Everyone is wrapped in blankets or furs. We have heaters, a giant wood fire, and we all sit in the afternoon sun and laugh. Such an incredible gift.

The next day, obliterate the garden.

Cutback week begins when the peony leaves turn red. At the

beginning of the book in mid-April, we had a full discussion on how to do cutbacks. As a quick review, remember to leave the ground covers alone. Just remove any dead flowers. For mounding plants cut them to 6" (15cm) round. And finally for the vast majority of upright growing plants, they should be cut down to 1"- 2" (2.5cm – 5cm). Ornamental tall grasses or sturdy perennials (*Echinacea, Rudbeckia, etc.*) should be left up for winter interest. A good rule of thumb is that if plants flower in mid to late September then don't cut them back. This will allow them to remain strong through the winter.

Tall Ornamental grass, e.g. Karl Forester Reed Grass, or *Echinacea*, or *Rudbeckia*

Often, I up-light my perennials, especially grasses, with my lighting system because I like to see the movement throughout the winter.

Hydrangea 'Pinky WInky' Up-lit

You do not have to cut back in the fall, though. Cutbacks can also be done in mid-April. I do have a couple of caveats on this. If you have any disease or pest issues, then I highly recommend cutting back so that you remove any possible leaf litter that may harbour over-wintering eggs or spores. The other caveat is a human trait. In the spring, people just want to see things spring up in the garden. They are looking at new varieties or new furniture or just being outside and marveling at the big yellow ball in the sky that has only suddenly appeared in the horizon after six months. Having to deal with last year's work and debris often puts a bit of a cloud on your exuberance for the new season.

We have quite a large garden, so the best method we have found for doing cutbacks is to put a large tarp on the ground. Throw all of the cutting on it, drag the tarp to the truck, toss it in, and then take everything to the eco-station. If you have a composter, then a shredder is a fantastic device as it will reduce the bulk and speed up the composting process. Ensure that you keep a few bags as "browns," if you continue to add to the composter in the winter.

Bagging is usually what most people do, but please ensure you keep the weight down. If you can't lift the bag then the waste management people will struggle as well. If anything, gardeners are known for being a compassionate group.

Once done, blow all of the remaining leaves onto the lawn and either rake or mow it up and keep the clean leaves for Halloween.

Absolutely, though, any twinge of worry from your subconscious mind that there is disease or pests, bag it and toss it.

All cutbacks must be finished before Oct 22. Even this date is pushing it. When winter comes, sometimes he stays for good.

Week 3 in October – Preparing the Garden for Winter

Preparing for the winter always starts with the soil. Once all of the leaves have been cutback then you can see the soil. If you have larger spaces in the perennial garden, an annual garden, or vegetable garden it is a good idea to take a shovel or spade and dig down at least six inches and turn over the soil. You don't have to break up the lumps as the idea is to expose any eggs that have been laid to the winter's killing cold. Also, this opens up the soil and allows more oxygen to penetrate deep into the earth. I do know many people that also add their amendments at this time. You can usually buy them on sale, but also it saves time from having to purchase and spread in the middle of a very busy spring. Here again just be mindful of leaf diseases. Ensure that everything has been removed first so that you are not burying fungal diseases under your amendments.

Once that is complete, then you will need to turn your attention to ponds, waterfalls, and water features. Running water from a waterfall will continue to operate until about

minus seven Celsius. Although, one year I went to bed and woke up to minus fourteen and the waterfall was still fine. However, I wouldn't recommend that. Pumps need to be pulled out and put in the house or garage for the winter. Just as with your irrigation system any water that freezes in the pump can potentially damage it. Water features, for example, bird baths or tiered fountains should be covered with a tarp. It can crack if ice forms, but also the dyes used in the concrete, or especially, in plastic can fade over time. Of course, you will drain your feature as well.

Now with ponds and fish, you can keep them outside if your pond is a proper depth, at least two feet (60cm). You will stop feeding your fish in mid-October as the fish are not able to digest properly in cold water. You will need another pump that isn't too strong but enough to create a small burble in the water. This will keep the water oxygenated through the winter. And then you will need a pond heater. They are usually sold at

 greenhouses that sell pond supplies. I had fairly hardy goldfish and kept my fish outside for many years, the larger ones always made it but some of the smaller ones were hit and

miss. I kept my heater on a timer so that ice formed on the surface of the pond except for around the burbler, and then used a rubber pond liner for extra insulation whenever it got down into the depths of the minus twenties and thirties. Because you do have moving water, you will have evaporation and therefore you will need to top up the pond periodically. My pond was small so I had to top up every couple of weeks.

Week 4 in October – Wrapping and Watering

If you listen to the radio, all of the gardening gurus will be sounding the alarm to get outside and water in all of the trees and shrubs. The plant material will essentially be entering a five-month drought. Once the surface soil freezes, it is difficult for the roots to access any water. By watering deeply at the end of October, you place easily accessible water near the root.

For new trees, water at the base for 20 min

One of the best ways to water is to use a Ross Watering rod. It is a long metal rod that is attached to the garden hose. It usually comes with a fertilizer attachment. Don't use the attachment as you don't want in any way to re-stimulate the plant this late in the season. For larger trees you will want to plunge the rod about 1 ½' (45cm) down. But you don't put the rod at the base of the plant. Rather you put the rod just under the outer edge of the canopy of the tree. This is called the drip line. The large roots that are near the base of the tree are for stability and for storage.

For shrubs water for 1 minute

The fine thin roots out at the outer edge of the canopy are where the feeder roots are and those are the roots that will collect water and nutrients. For Shrubs, you only need to go down 6" to 1' (15cm to 30cm). And again the same, put the rod around the outer edge of the canopy as well. In general, I recommend about 3 minutes to 5 minutes per shrub with about 3 holes (1 minute per hole), for trees 20 minutes to an hour per tree with 5 to 10 minutes per hole. You can always water longer but this will help immeasurably. If you have large groupings of trees and shrubs, then using a sprinkler or soaker hose to soak the bed will work fine. Provided, that you don't let the water run off the bed and down the street.

Wrapping

Once all of the plants have been watered in, then it is time to start wrapping the base of the trees.

Tender zone 4 trees can be wrapped once the leaves have fallen. Mouse or rabbit activity can be quite devastating by the spring. Once the snow falls, it insulates the soil underneath and allows the vermin to tunnel underneath and eat the sod or eat at the base of soft barked trees, example fruit trees, like apples and cherries. You can buy plastic tree guards or use cut up weeping tile to collar the base of young trees. If you have higher snowfall areas then you may need to use chicken wire and wrap up the trunks of the

trees to prevent rabbits, beaver, or moose and deer. In general, older trees have a heavy bark that protects the plants but if the animals are hungry enough they will eat anything.

For tall shrubs, specifically cedars, don't wrap them just yet but do push 3 poles into the ground while the soil is still soft and not frozen. For the last few years experts have not been recommending wrapping burlap or snow fabrics directly on to cedars. It is better to put three or four poles around the shrub and then wrap the burlap around the poles so that there is an air space between the shrub and fabric. After, a cedar has been in for two years, it should be safe enough not to wrap for the winter, provided they have been thoroughly watered at the end of October. If a site is protected, i.e., not on the bald prairie, I often recommend wrapping in late February. As it is usually the sun damage in the spring that causes the most amount of damage.

There are only a few beautiful sunny warm days left. Ensure that you grab a cup of tea whenever you can and sit out in the sun and be a kitty, eyes closed and nose turned up to the sun.

November

Week 1 in November – Covering Tender Shrubs

By now, the ground should be crusty on top, at least in the mornings. And is a perfect time to start covering the tender zone 4 shrubs.

Roses

Roses that need to be covered are any of the Zone 4 and higher hybrid teas and floribundas. The prairies have wonderful roses as well, and our roses are amazingly hardy, especially those roses developed out of Saskatchewan and Manitoba. Just as a generalization though, usually roses sold from greenhouses are winter hardy, and those sold from box stores are often less hardy. Primarily, because of cost. Stores can buy large sized roses at a low cost from Portland or Vancouver. Zone 5 roses grow incredibly fast in comparison to our slower growing Zone 3 hardy roses.

If you cover your tender roses through the winter, you will have much greater success in getting them to live through the winter. In most of the hardware stores and greenhouses, they sell Styrofoam rose covers. Buy the larger ones. When you get home, prune your roses so that they will fit inside the Styrofoam cone. Put the cone over the rose and cut a hole in the top of the cone. Take peat moss and fill the Styrofoam cone up to the top, completely burying the rose. I then put a piece of landscape fabric or snow fabric on top of the hole to prevent moisture from getting in and wetting the peat moss. You can also use a peat moss tree pot. I don't recommend a cardboard boxes because it can turn to mush if we get a good rainstorm during the middle of winter. And plastic is not advisable because it creates too much temperature fluctuations through the summer. The point of the cap is to reduce temperature fluctuations, and protect the buds.

You will then take the Styrofoam cap off in mid-April and two weeks later pull the peat moss away from the roses and use that as an amendment for the soil.

Other Zone 4 Shrubs

Rhododendrons need their buds protected over winter

For other Zone 4 plants like boxwood, Rhododendrons, azalea, and some globe cedars you can use pop up tents that are now becoming quite popular. Here, I still cut a hole at the top of them. What I do is not to fill them up  with peat moss but with dry leaves or bark mulch. The dry leaves can be saved for the spring for   adding to your compost or bark chip can be used to spread on your shrub beds. The dry leaves help in protecting the tender flower buds of plants like the rhododendrons and azaleas. What the tents do is prevent sun scald in the early spring. Sun scald is basically the same as the bad sun burn that skiers get during spring skiing. To the plant it is just as painful. The bark is badly injured and will eventually peal or potentially become infected

 For your tender perennials, or perennials that you think just have a hard time getting up in the morning, it is a good idea to put

a cone of peat moss on them and make sure they are covered in snow through the winter.

As for the tall cedars, on the prairies the first 2 years are very hard on young cedars. They are not meant to grow here and will often badly sunscald in the spring. The sunlight bounces off the snow and sun burns the leaves. Once a leaf is sun burnt, it doesn't come back. To prevent sunscald, you can wrap the cedars in burlap or other snow fabrics. At the end of October, I had you put in tall stakes around your young cedars. You can now wrap the cedars with the fabric. The point of the fabric isn't to keep them warm but rather to reduce the drying effects of the wind and reduce the glare from the snow. If you want to see your evergreens through the winter, then as long as you cover your evergreens before March they will be fine.

Elm tree pruning can now begin. Because of Dutch Elm

Disease you can only prune elms between November 1st and March 31st. Once all of the leaves have dropped off your trees you can start pruning now. I would, however, recommend that you hold off pruning fruit trees until late March early April as the winter winds can severely dry out your cuts and potentially harm the trees.

Tools can be brought inside and should be oiled to protect the blades. You are supposed to sharpen them and clean them first. In all of my hundreds of courses that I have taught over the years not once have I actually done that. But I highly recommend that you should.

Bring in any liquid fertilizers, pesticides etc. so that they do not freeze. They will lose their potency.

Week 2 in November – Winter Containers

Winter pots are just a great activity to do in the beginning of November. What we like to do is go out hiking or into the forest and collect spruce, dogwood, birch branches, rose hips and pine and then bring that home for winter arrangements.

Fill a black plastic 2-gallon or 5-gallon pot with wet peat moss or sand. Create a cone of chicken wire and put that on top of the sand.

First, in the middle of the pot, push through the sand your large branches of birch or dogwood.

Then stick the evergreen branches through the chicken wire

into the sand. In the middle of the pot, around the birch branches, put in smaller dog wood followed with fill from the rose hips and pine. Then, *voila*, you have a fantastic base for a winter arrangement. Add water and then let it freeze in over-night. Most of the greenhouses will carry greens and other ornaments that can be used to create beautiful winter pots or they have courses as well. These arrangements will last right through to the end of February. If you use cedar bows or pine you will find that they start to brown off in late January but can be easily removed.

There is only one last thing to do. And that is to plan an amazing winter get away, order new plant catalogues, and dream about next spring. Thank you so much for being on this garden journey with me.

Kevin K. Napora

Notes About the Author

Kevin Napora
Landscape Designer, Master Gardener, B.Sc. Agric.

Kevin Napora believes in the power of nature's aesthetic to inspire. Having spent close to a quarter century studying, landscaping, and designing residential gardens, Kevin created and maintained gardens that motivate, relax, and refresh. After receiving more than 12 industry awards in gardening (2 of which are for Residential Design in Alberta), and being sited in various magazines and newspapers, he ardently promotes his love for gardening through presentations to garden clubs, courses, and articles. Over the years, he has realized that a garden isn't a collection of plants and stone, but rather, a garden is a wholistic embodiment of the family living and enjoying the outdoor space with nature. Encouraging people, through thoughtful design and education, to experience the joys of the garden, is Kevin's passion.